AMERICAN EMPOWER

STUDENT'S BOOK B

WITH DIGITAL PACK

B1+

INTERMEDIATE

Adrian Doff, Craig Thaine
Herbert Puchta, Jeff Stranks, Peter Lewis-Jones
with Rachel Godfrey and Gareth Davies

 **CAMBRIDGE**

AMERICAN EMPOWER is a six-level general English course for adult and young adult learners, taking students from beginner to advanced level (CEFR A1 to C1). *American Empower* combines course content from Cambridge University Press with validated assessment from the experts at Cambridge Assessment English.

American Empower's unique mix of engaging classroom materials and reliable assessment enables learners to make consistent and measurable progress.

Content you'll love.

Assessment you

can trust.

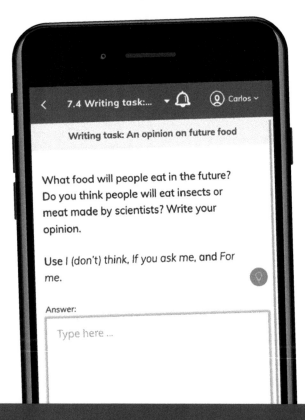

Better Learning with *American Empower*

Better Learning is our simple approach where **insights** we've gained from research have helped shape **content** that drives **results**.

Learner engagement

1 Content that informs and motivates

Insights
Sustained motivation is key to successful language learning and skills development.

Content
Clear learning goals, thought-provoking images, texts, and speaking activities, plus video content to arouse curiosity.

Results
Content that surprises, entertains, and provokes an emotional response, helping teachers to deliver motivating and memorable lessons.

6A YOU SHOULD WEAR GOOD WALKING SHOES

Learn to talk about advice and rules
- Modals of obligation
- Compound nouns

1 SPEAKING AND READING

a 💬 Discuss the questions.
1 What do you think the phrase "culture shock" means? What difficulties might culture shock cause?
2 Think of a country you would like to visit. How do you think it would be different from your own country? Think about the words in the box.

food   people   customs   getting around
cities and streets

b Quickly read the article about CultureMee, an app for tourists traveling to other countries. Which of the things below does the app provide?
1 "insider tips" about the culture
2 information about main tourist sites
3 a history of the country
4 detailed descriptions of famous buildings
5 lists of recommended hotels and restaurants
6 tips about how to behave in the country
7 information about local attitudes and customs

CULTURE SHOCK? THERE'S AN APP TO DEAL WITH THAT

Many travel apps and guidebooks can help you to book a cheap homestay or an expensive hotel with a swimming pool, and they can tell you where to go windsurfing or what restaurants serve the best seafood. But what if you want information on how to greet people politely in Tokyo, how much to tip a taxi driver in Madrid, or where to meet local people in Rio de Janeiro? Well, a new app for your cell phone can now do all that for you.

The app is called CultureMee, and it not only gives straightforward travel advice, but it also provides **insights** into the culture of the country you're visiting. It was set up by an Irish couple, John and Dee Lee, and has quickly grown in popularity. Thousands of people are already using the app, which now covers locations all over the world. It has also won several international awards.

The idea for the app came to them while they were on vacation in East Africa a few years ago. They had guidebooks that told them about places to visit, but they found it difficult to find out about what kind of plug they needed for their hair dryer or exactly what vaccinations they needed.

They realized that it would be very useful to have an app that could give people this kind of basic travel advice. They also wanted to help people understand the culture of any country they might visit, so this became an **integral** part of the app's content.

The couple decided not to take the conventional **approach to** culture, which is already a feature of standard guidebooks, but rather to focus on the everyday lives of people in the country. There are plenty

of apps available that can help you book vacations and places to stay, and that give you information about tourist sights and museums. However, John and Dee felt that most travel apps didn't focus on ordinary people, so they decided to put this **at the heart of** what CultureMee does.

CultureMee offers a wide range of cultural content, including background information about the country and its history, details on contemporary culture, and advice on dealing with "culture shock." Users can access videos, produced by the couple themselves, that **supplement** the core content of the app. Many of these give tips on how to engage with local people and how to behave in an appropriate way. They are based on interviews with people who have visited the country, and who can talk **with authority** about it from a visitor's point of view. There are also interviews with local people who provide insights into how they view their own culture.

So, imagine that someone from the U.S. wants to travel to Brazil. They can select the appropriate culture video and hear a Brazilian talking about Brazilian culture. They can also watch a video of a non-Brazilian person talking about how to get along with Brazilians and understand their culture. An essential aim of John and Dee's

project is to create an online community of people who are interested in travel and culture. As the app becomes more popular, they hope this community will continue to augment* it with their own stories and viewpoints.

*augment (v) to increase the size or value of something by adding to it

A screenshot from CultureMee

John and Dee Lee, founders of CultureMee

c Read the article again. Decide if the sentences are true (T) or false (F). Find phrases in the text that tell you the answer.
1 The new app only gives cultural advice, not practical travel advice.
2 CultureMee has already been successful.
3 John and Dee's guidebook on East Africa didn't tell them everything they needed to know.
4 John and Dee decided to interview ordinary people who know about a country.
5 All the interviews are with people who come from the country they talk about.
6 They would like people who use the app to contribute to it and improve it.

d What do the words in bold mean in the context of the article? Choose a or b.
1 **insights**
  a knowledge of something
  b suggested places to visit
2 **integral**
  a additional, extra
  b central, essential
3 **approach to**
  a information about
  b way of looking at
4 **at the heart of**
  a feeling strongly about something
  b central to something
5 **supplement**
  a add to something
  b use instead of something
6 **with authority**
  a knowledgeable about something
  b having permission to talk about something

2 VOCABULARY Compound nouns

a Read the information below about compound nouns, then underline the compound nouns in the title and introduction to the article on p. 68.

Compound nouns combine two words. We write some compound nouns as one word (e.g., *lunchtime*) and others as two words (e.g., *living room*). They are usually formed by:
- noun + noun (e.g., *newspaper*)
- verb + -ing + noun (e.g., *washing machine*)
- noun + verb + -ing (e.g., *ice skating*)

b 🔊 01.03 **Pronunciation** Listen to the compound nouns from the article. Which part is stressed – the first or the second word? Practice saying the words.

c Complete the compound nouns with the words in the box.

book   screen   insect   pack   shop   baseball   tour   walking

1 _____ guide
2 sun_____
3 souvenir _____
4 _____ cap
5 _____ back
6 _____ guide
7 _____ shoes
8 _____ repellent

UNIT 6

The Ruins of Tikal: Insider Tips

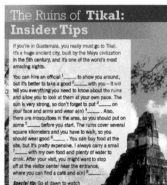

If you're in Guatemala, you really must go to Tikal. It's a huge ancient city, built by the Maya civilization in the 5th century, and it's one of the world's most amazing sights.

You can hire an official ¹_____ to show you around, but it's better to take a good ²_____ with you – it will tell you everything you need to know about the ruins and allow you to look at them at your own pace. The sun is very strong, so don't forget to put ³_____ on your face and arms and wear a(n) ⁴_____ . Also, there are mosquitoes in the area, so you should put on some ⁵_____ before you start. The ruins cover several square kilometers and you have to walk, so you should wear good ⁶_____ . You can buy food at the site, but it's pretty expensive. I always carry a small ⁷_____ with my own food and plenty of water to drink. After your visit, you might want to stop off at the visitor center near the entrance, where you can find a café and a(n) ⁸_____ .

Special tip: Go at dawn to watch the sun rise over the ruins. It's an experience you'll never forget!

d Read the travel tips for Tikal in Guatemala. Complete the text with compound nouns from 2c.

e ⤢ Communication 6A 💬 Student A: Go to p. 130. Student B: Go to p. 132.

3 LISTENING

a 💬 Look at the photos and the information about Kim, Will, and Daniel. What cultural differences do you think they noticed when they lived overseas? Compare your ideas with other students.

Kim from Canada went to live in Ecuador.

Will from the U.S. worked for a company in Nigeria.

Daniel from Brazil went to live in the U.S.

---

2 Personalized and relevant

Insights
Language learners benefit from frequent opportunities to personalize their responses.

Content
Personalization tasks in every unit make the target language more meaningful to the individual learner.

Results
Personal responses make learning more memorable and inclusive, with all students participating in spontaneous spoken interaction.

> "There are so many adjectives to describe such a wonderful series, but in my opinion it's very reliable, practical, and modern."
>
> **Zenaide Brianez, Director of Studies, Instituto da Língua Inglesa, Brazil**

Measurable progress

1 Assessment you can trust

Insights
Tests developed and validated by Cambridge Assessment English, the world leaders in language assessment, to ensure they are accurate and meaningful.

Content
End-of-unit tests, mid- and end-of-course competency tests, and personalized CEFR test report forms provide reliable information on progress with language skills.

Results
Teachers can see learners' progress at a glance, and learners can see measurable progress, which leads to greater motivation.

Results of an impact study showing % improvement of Reading levels, based on global *Empower* students' scores over one year.

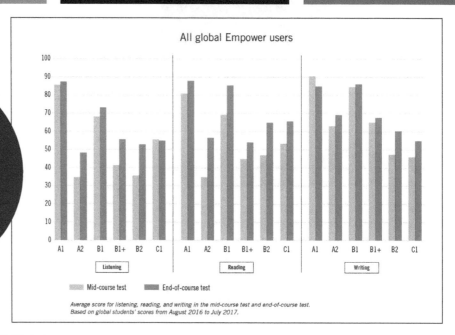

All global Empower users

Mid-course test End-of-course test

Listening   Reading   Writing

Average score for listening, reading, and writing in the mid-course test and end-of-course test.
Based on global students' scores from August 2016 to July 2017.

Cambridge English Empower B1+ intermediate
Competency test
Estimated CEFR level

Student Name:
Report Date:
You are now at the level to prepare for *Cambridge English: PET*

Skill
End of course level indicator

Overall
Reading
Listening
Writing
Speaking

Close to B1   B1 level   Good performance   Strong performance

Competency

Please note:
The Mid-course level indicator is replaced by the End-of-course level indicator.
The Reading, Listening and Writing sections are automatically scored. The score for the Speaking section is entered by your teacher.

CAMBRIDGE UNIVERSITY PRESS

Cambridge Assessment English

> *We started using the tests provided with* Empower *and our students started showing better results from this point until now.*

Kristina Ivanova, Director of Foreign Language Training Centre, ITMO University, Saint Petersburg, Russia

2 Evidence of impact

Insights
Schools and colleges need to show that they are evaluating the effectiveness of their language programs.

Content
Empower (British English) impact studies have been carried out in various countries, including Russia, Brazil, Turkey, and the UK, to provide evidence of positive impact and progress.

Results
Colleges and universities have demonstrated a significant improvement in language level between the mid- and end-of-course tests, as well as a high level of teacher satisfaction with *Empower*.

Manageable learning

1 Mobile friendly

Insights
Learners expect online content to be mobile friendly but also flexible and easy to use on any digital device.

Content
American Empower provides easy access to Digital Workbook content that works on any device and includes practice activities with audio.

Results
Digital Workbook content is easy to access anywhere, and produces meaningful and actionable data so teachers can track their students' progress and adapt their lesson accordingly.

> *I had been studying English for 10 years before university, and I didn't succeed. But now with Empower I know my level of English has changed.*

Nikita, *Empower* Student, ITMO University, Saint Petersburg, Russia

2 Corpus-informed

Insights
Corpora can provide valuable information about the language items learners are able to learn successfully at each CEFR level.

Content
Two powerful resources – Cambridge Corpus and English Profile – informed the development of the *Empower* course syllabus and the writing of the materials.

Results
Learners are presented with the target language they are able to incorporate and use at the right point in their learning journey. They are not overwhelmed with unrealistic learning expectations.

Rich in practice

1 Language in use

Insights
It is essential that learners are offered frequent and manageable opportunities to practice the language they have been focusing on.

Content
Throughout the *American Empower* Student's Book, learners are offered a wide variety of practice activities, plenty of controlled practice, and frequent opportunities for communicative spoken practice.

Results
Meaningful practice makes new language more memorable and leads to more efficient progress in language acquisition.

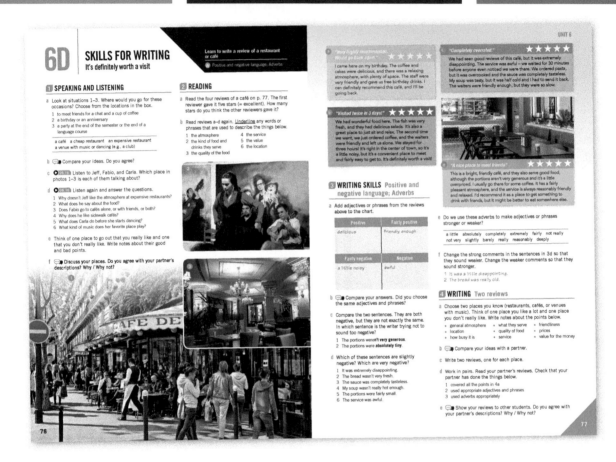

2 Beyond the classroom

Insights
Progress with language learning often requires work outside of the classroom, and different teaching models require different approaches.

Content
American Empower is available with a print workbook, online practice, documentary-style videos that expose learners to real-world English, plus additional resources with extra ideas and fun activities.

Results
This choice of additional resources helps teachers to find the most effective ways to motivate their students both inside and outside the classroom.

Unit overview

Unit Opener

Getting started page – Clear learning objectives to give an immediate sense of purpose.

Lessons A and B

Grammar and Vocabulary – Input and practice of core grammar and vocabulary, plus a mix of skills.

Digital Workbook (online, mobile): Grammar and Vocabulary

Lesson C

Everyday English – Functional language in common, everyday situations.

Digital Workbook (online, mobile): Listening and Speaking

Unit Progress Test

Lesson D

Integrated Skills – Practice of all four skills, with a special emphasis on writing.

Digital Workbook (online, mobile): Reading and Writing

Review

Extra practice of grammar, vocabulary, and pronunciation. Also a "Review your progress" section for students to reflect on the unit.

Mid- / End-of-course test

Additional practice

Further practice is available for outside of the class with these components.

Digital Workbook (online, mobile)

Workbook (printed)

Components

Resources – Available on cambridgeone.org

- Audio
- Video
- Unit Progress Tests (Print)
- Unit Progress Tests (Online)

- Mid- and end-of-course assessment (Print)
- Mid- and end-of-course assessment (Online)

- Digital Workbook (Online)
- Photocopiable Grammar, Vocabulary, and Pronunciation worksheets

CONTENTS

4

This page is intentionally left blank.

 CAN DO OBJECTIVES

- Talk about advice and rules
- Describe food
- Ask for and give recommendations
- Write a review of a restaurant or café

UNIT **6**

DIFFERENT CULTURES

GETTING STARTED

a 💬 Look at the photo. Ask and answer the questions.

1 In which part of the world do you think the photo was taken?
2 What job are the men doing?
3 How is this similar to or different from the same job in your culture?
4 Are there any jobs in your country that still use traditional methods? Give details.

b 💬 Have you met people from different cultures? If you have, what did you have in common? How were you different? If you haven't, what do you think they would find interesting or surprising about your country's culture?

6A | YOU SHOULD WEAR GOOD WALKING SHOES

1 SPEAKING AND READING

a 💬📢 Discuss the questions.

1 What do you think the phrase "culture shock" means? What difficulties might culture shock cause?

2 Think of a country you would like to visit. How do you think it would be different from your own country? Think about the words in the box.

> food people customs getting around cities and streets

b Quickly read the article about CultureMee, an app for tourists traveling to other countries. Which of the things below does the app provide?

1 "insider tips" about the culture
2 information about main tourist sites
3 a history of the country
4 detailed descriptions of famous buildings
5 lists of recommended hotels and restaurants
6 tips about how to behave in the country
7 information about local attitudes and customs

CULTURE SHOCK? THERE'S AN APP TO DEAL WITH THAT

Many travel apps and guidebooks can help you to book a cheap homestay or an expensive hotel with a swimming pool, and they can tell you where to go windsurfing or what restaurants serve the best seafood. But what if you want information on how to greet people politely in Tokyo, how much to tip a taxi driver in Madrid, or where to meet local people in Rio de Janeiro? Well, a new app for your cell phone can now do all that for you.

The app is called CultureMee, and it not only gives straightforward travel advice, but it also provides **insights** into the culture of the country you're visiting. It was set up by an Irish couple, John and Dee Lee, and has quickly grown in popularity. Thousands of people are already using the app, which now covers locations all over the world. It has also won several international awards.

The idea for the app came to them while they were on vacation in East Africa a few years ago. They had guidebooks that told them about places to visit, but they found it difficult to find out about what kind of plug they needed for their hair dryer or exactly what vaccinations they needed.

They realized that it would be very useful to have an app that could give people this kind of basic travel advice. They also wanted to help people understand the culture of any country they might visit, so this became an **integral** part of the app's content.

The couple decided not to take the conventional **approach to** culture, which is already a feature of standard guidebooks, but rather to focus on the everyday lives of people in the country. There are plenty of apps available that can help you book vacations and places to stay, and that give you information about tourist sights and museums. However, John and Dee felt that most travel apps didn't focus on ordinary people, so they decided to put this **at the heart of** what CultureMee does.

CultureMee offers a wide range of cultural content, including background information about the country and its history, details on contemporary culture, and advice on dealing with "culture shock." Users can access videos, produced by the couple themselves, that **supplement** the core content of the app. Many of these give tips on how to engage with local people and how to behave in an appropriate way. They are based on interviews with people who have visited the country, and who can talk **with authority** about it from a visitor's point of view. There are also interviews with local people who provide insights into how they view their own culture.

So, imagine that someone from the U.S. wants to travel to Brazil. They can select the appropriate culture video and hear a Brazilian talking about Brazilian culture. They can also watch a video of a non-Brazilian person talking about how to get along with Brazilians and understand their culture.

An essential aim of John and Dee's project is to create an online community of people who are interested in travel and culture. As the app becomes more popular, they hope this community will continue to augment* it with their own stories and viewpoints.

***augment** (v) to increase the size or value of something by adding to it

A screenshot from CultureMee

John and Dee Lee, founders of CultureMee

68

c Read the article again. Decide if the sentences are true (T) or false (F). Find phrases in the text that tell you the answer.

1 The new app only gives cultural advice, not practical travel advice.
2 CultureMee has already been successful.
3 John and Dee's guidebook on East Africa didn't tell them everything they needed to know.
4 John and Dee decided to interview ordinary people who know about a country.
5 All the interviews are with people who come from the country they talk about.
6 They would like people who use the app to contribute to it and improve it.

d What do the words in **bold** mean in the context of the article? Choose a or b.

1 **insights**
   a knowledge of something
   b suggested places to visit
2 **integral**
   a additional, extra
   b central, essential
3 **approach to**
   a information about
   b way of looking at
4 **at the heart of**
   a feeling strongly about something
   b central to something
5 **supplement**
   a add to something
   b use instead of something
6 **with authority**
   a knowledgeable about something
   b having permission to talk about something

2 VOCABULARY Compound nouns

a Read the information below about compound nouns, then underline the compound nouns in the title and introduction to the article on p. 68.

> Compound nouns combine two words. We write some compound nouns as one word (e.g., *lunchtime*) and others as two words (e.g., *living room*). They are usually formed by:
> • noun + noun (e.g., *newspaper*)
> • verb + -ing + noun (e.g., *washing machine*)
> • noun + verb + -ing (e.g., *ice skating*)

b ▶06.01 **Pronunciation** Listen to the compound nouns from the article. Which part is stressed – the first or the second word? Practice saying the words.

c Complete the compound nouns with the words in the box.

book   screen   insect   pack   shop   baseball   tour   walking

1 _____ guide   5 back_____
2 sun_____   6 guide_____
3 souvenir _____   7 _____ shoes
4 _____ cap   8 _____ repellent

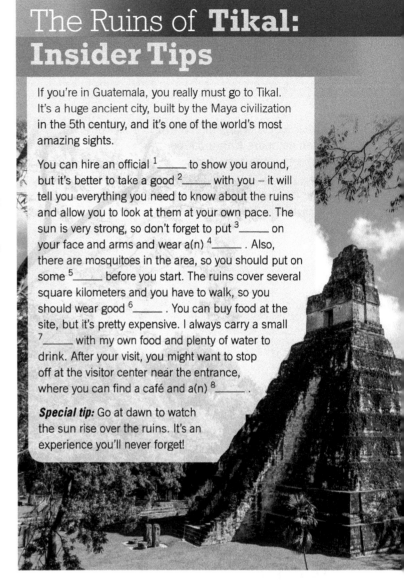

The Ruins of **Tikal:** Insider Tips

If you're in Guatemala, you really must go to Tikal. It's a huge ancient city, built by the Maya civilization in the 5th century, and it's one of the world's most amazing sights.

You can hire an official [1]_____ to show you around, but it's better to take a good [2]_____ with you – it will tell you everything you need to know about the ruins and allow you to look at them at your own pace. The sun is very strong, so don't forget to put [3]_____ on your face and arms and wear a(n) [4]_____ . Also, there are mosquitoes in the area, so you should put on some [5]_____ before you start. The ruins cover several square kilometers and you have to walk, so you should wear good [6]_____ . You can buy food at the site, but it's pretty expensive. I always carry a small [7]_____ with my own food and plenty of water to drink. After your visit, you might want to stop off at the visitor center near the entrance, where you can find a café and a(n) [8]_____ .

Special tip: Go at dawn to watch the sun rise over the ruins. It's an experience you'll never forget!

d Read the travel tips for Tikal in Guatemala. Complete the text with compound nouns from 2c.

e ≫ Communication 6A 💬 Student A: Go to p. 130. Student B: Go to p. 132.

3 LISTENING

a 💬 Look at the photos and the information about Kim, Will, and Daniel. What cultural differences do you think they noticed when they lived overseas? Compare your ideas with other students.

Kim from Canada went to live in Ecuador.

Will from the U.S. worked for a company in Nigeria.

Daniel from Brazil went to live in the U.S.

b ▶️06.02 Listen to Kim, Will, and Daniel. Which of these topics do they talk about? One topic is not mentioned.

> talking to people   being on time   children
> making eye contact   getting up early   going to bed

c ▶️06.02 Listen again and write notes in the chart. Then compare with a partner.

Country	Cultural difference	Example(s)	Comments they make about it
Ecuador			
Nigeria			
U.S.			

d 💬 Think about the three cultural differences in the chart. Have you ever been in similar situations? What happened?

4 GRAMMAR Modals of obligation

a Complete these sentences from the interviews with the words in the box. You will use some of the words more than once.

> can   can't   have to   don't have to   must
> must not   should   shouldn't

Kim
1 If a meeting starts at 10 o'clock, you _____ be there at 10:00. You _____ come maybe fifteen or twenty minutes later, and that's fine.
2 They expect me to come on time, and they always say, "You _____ be late. You _____ come on time."

Will
3 If you're talking to someone you don't know well, you _____ look right at them.
4 In the U.S., you _____ definitely look the other person in the eye when you talk.

Daniel
5 At a certain time, maybe 7:00 or 8:00, all the children _____ go to bed.
6 In Brazil, children _____ usually stay up as long as they want. ... They _____ go to bed at a fixed time.
7 I think children _____ join in the life of the family, and it's a pity if they _____ be part of it.

b ▶️06.03 Listen and check your answers.

c ≫ Now go to Grammar Focus 6A on p. 154.

d Complete these rules about transportation in your country. Use the modals in the box.

> must   have to   need to   don't have to   don't need to
> must not   should   shouldn't   can   can't

Buses
1 You _____ buy a ticket in advance.
2 You _____ buy a ticket on the bus.

Walking and cycling
3 You _____ use a crosswalk when you want to cross the street.
4 You _____ wear a bike helmet.
5 You _____ ride a bike on the sidewalk.
 You _____ use bike lanes.

Cars
6 Passengers _____ wear a seat belt.
7 You _____ drive with your lights on during the day.

Taxis
8 You _____ stop taxis in the street.
9 You _____ book taxis in advance.
10 You _____ give taxi drivers a tip.

e A foreign visitor is coming to live in your country for six months. Prepare to give them some advice. Use the ideas in the box and your own ideas to make a list of rules and tips.

> roads, sidewalks, and bike lanes   public transportation
> eating and drinking   going out at night   clothes
> talking to people who are older than you   language
> parks and public spaces

You shouldn't eat or drink when walking in the street. You should always give your seat to an older passenger on the bus.

f 💬 Take turns reading your rules and tips aloud. Discuss the questions.
1 Which rules and tips are about safety?
2 Which are about being polite to people?
3 Which rules and tips are the most important?

5 SPEAKING

a Work with a partner. Think about a foreign culture you both know something about. How is it different from your culture? Think about these topics and write brief notes.

> children   meals   time   men and women
> older people   greetings   how people dress

b 💬 Work in groups. Tell your group about the differences in the culture you chose. Ask the other students questions about the culture they chose. Do you agree with them?

6B | IT'S TASTIER THAN I EXPECTED

Learn to describe food

- **G** Comparatives and superlatives
- **V** Describing food

1 VOCABULARY Describing food

a 💬 Look at photos a–e and discuss the questions.

1 Which food would you most like to eat?
2 What country do you think each dish comes from?
3 What ingredients does each dish contain?
4 Which of the dishes could a vegetarian eat?

b Match descriptions 1–5 with photos a–e.

1 tasty Moroccan meatballs cooked in a tomato sauce, served with couscous and fresh herbs
2 creamy Mexican avocado and tomato dip with crunchy tortilla chips
3 whitefish cooked in a spicy Thai sauce with hot green chilies
4 Japanese noodles with vegetables in a light soup served with an egg
5 a slice of rich Austrian chocolate cake with a bitter orange filling

c Which adjectives in 1b could you use to describe a salad, a bowl of soup, or a curry dish?

d ≫ Now go to Vocabulary Focus 6B on p. 137.

e ▶06.08 **Pronunciation** Listen and repeat these words. Pay attention to the pronunciation of the letters *sh* and *ch*.

/ʃ/	/tʃ/
fre<u>sh</u>	<u>ch</u>ocolate
ma<u>sh</u>	<u>ch</u>op
<u>sh</u>ip	ri<u>ch</u>
<u>sh</u>ape	crun<u>ch</u>y

f 💬 A visitor has come to your town. You're going to give advice about where to eat and what typical dishes to try.

Student A: Give the visitor advice.
Student B: You are the visitor. Listen and ask further questions.

g 💬 Now change roles and have a second conversation.

2 LISTENING

a 💬 Look at the photo on the right and discuss the questions.

1 Do you have vending machines in your country? What do they sell?
2 How often do you use them? What do you usually buy?

b ▶06.09 Listen to part of a radio show about vending machines in Japan.

1 What types of food and drink are mentioned?
2 What are the advantages for customers of vending machines over buying things from a store?
3 What does the reporter think of the hot meal?

c 💬 Would you buy hot food from a vending machine? Why / Why not?

3 GRAMMAR Comparatives and superlatives

a ▶ 06.10 Complete the sentences with the words in the box. Then listen and check your answers.

as good as   a little longer than   the best by far   the highest   much better than   much cheaper

1 Japan has _____ number of vending machines per person in the world.
2 It's _____ for sellers to run a vending machine than a store.
3 But is curry and rice from a machine _____ curry and rice from a restaurant?
4 It's taking _____ I imagined.
5 It's actually _____ I expected.
6 I think it might be _____ vending machine meal I've ever eaten.

b ⫸ Now go to Grammar Focus 6B on p. 154.

c Use the ideas below to write sentences with comparatives, superlatives, and (not) as … as.

cheap   fun   good for you   healthy interesting   nice   spicy   sweet   tasty

- dark chocolate / milk chocolate / white chocolate
- street food / food in expensive restaurants / homemade food
- Japanese food / Mexican food / Indian food
- vegetarian food / meat dishes / fish dishes
- food from my country / food from other countries
- eating alone / eating with friends

Milk chocolate isn't as healthy as dark chocolate.

d 💬🗣 Read your sentences aloud. Do you agree or disagree with each other?

"Have You Eaten?" May 13th

Singaporeans are my kind of people – they're passionate about food and eating!

People here eat often – they have five or six meals a day. Instead of "Hello" or "How are you?" they ask, "Have you eaten?" And it's hard to believe just how many different kinds of dishes you can get in this tiny country – Chinese, Indian, Arabic, European, and many, many more.

The best meal of the day today was lunch. The main course was *muri ghonto* or fish head curry – far more delicious than it sounds! It's a southern Indian dish. You can have it with rice, but we had it the way the Chinese do, with a soft bread roll.

Dessert was *cendol* – coconut milk, ice, and green noodles. It's a typical Southeast Asian dish. It wasn't as sweet as I expected, but the noodles were terrific – a little like jelly.

There are places to eat here to suit everyone – from food stalls in shopping malls to more upscale (and more expensive!) restaurants. My plan is to try as many as I can in the short time I'm here.

4 READING

a 💬🗣 Look at the photo on the left. Which country do you think it is?

b Read the blog "Hungry Adventures." Check your answer to 4a.

c Read the blog again. Find the descriptions of the dishes and match them with the food photos a–d.

1 ☐ chicken *satay*   3 ☐ *cendol*
2 ☐ *muri ghonto*   4 ☐ *thosai*

d 💬🗣 Discuss the questions.

1 Did the blog writer enjoy the dishes in 4c?
2 Which of the dishes would you like to try?

Traveling and Eating Around the World

Hawker Centers – Street Food, but Not on the Streets
May 14th

Singapore is famous for its street food, but it's been illegal to sell cooked food in the streets for many years. So, if you're looking for Singapore's famous street food, hawker centers are the places to go. These are indoor food courts with stalls that sell freshly cooked food. You choose your hawker stall according to what kind of cuisine you want – Thai, Malay, Chinese, Indian, Japanese, or Korean.

I went to the Golden Mile Food Center – it was amazing to see so many different food stalls under one roof. *Sup tulang*, a Malay-Indian dish of beef bones in a red spicy sauce, looked very tasty. But in the end I wanted something lighter, so I chose *ayam buah keluak*, a Paranakan (Chinese-Malay) dish. It's chicken with Indonesian black nuts, served with steamed rice. A good choice – one of the most unusual dishes I've ever tasted.

Little India, Big Appetite
May 15th

This part of Singapore was full of the sights and smells of India. I ate *thosai* – crispy Indian pancakes made from rice and lentils. They were served with rich and spicy dips and vegetable curry. The meal was light and fresh – delicious!

Still full from my Indian lunch, I explored the Arab Quarter. There was plenty of great food available, but sadly I wasn't hungry! I'll have to come back to Singapore. I didn't have a chance to explore Chinatown either.

By the evening I was hungry again, so I tried some of the barbecued food at Lau Pa Sat, an old market. I went for Malaysian chicken *satay*, pieces of chicken on sticks served with spicy peanut sauce. Absolutely delicious!

e Read the blog again and answer the questions.

1 What two habits show that the people in Singapore love food?
2 What did the blog writer eat with her fish head curry?
3 Why can't you buy cooked food on the street in Singapore?
4 Why didn't she have *sup tulang* at the Golden Mile Food Center?
5 Why didn't she eat anything in the Arab Quarter?
6 Which area of Singapore did she not go to?

f 💬 Imagine you are visiting Singapore. Where will you go? What will you eat?

> I'd really like to go to a big hawker center, so we can see all the different options.

5 SPEAKING

a You are going to talk about a special meal. Write notes about one of these meals. Use the ideas in the box to help you plan what to say.

- the most special meal you've ever made
- the most delicious meal you've ever eaten
- a meal you'll never forget

where?   when?   who with?   ingredients?
how was the food cooked?   taste, smell, color?

b 💬 Take turns describing your meals. Then talk about which of the meals sounds the most delicious.

> The most delicious meal I've ever eaten was in a little restaurant near my grandparents' house. I ate …

6C EVERYDAY ENGLISH
Well, what would you recommend?

1 LISTENING

a 💬🔊 Discuss the questions.

1 Which of these do you think is the best birthday present? Why?
- flowers
- dinner at a restaurant
- a homemade meal
- a book
- an expensive gift (e.g., jewelry)

2 Have you ever given these things to anyone?

b 💬🔊 Michael and his sister Vanessa are shopping for a gift for Michael's wife, Julia. What do you think Vanessa might recommend? Look at the examples in 1a and add some new ideas of your own.

c ▶06.12 Listen to Part 1. Does Vanessa mention your ideas?

d ▶06.12 Listen again. Are the sentences true (T) or false (F)?

1 Michael knows what to get Julia.
2 Michael thinks a book is a good idea.
3 Vanessa thinks Michael should get Julia something that matches her style.
4 Vanessa thinks Michael should let Julia choose something.

e 💬🔊 Do you agree with Vanessa's advice? What should Michael get Julia?

2 USEFUL LANGUAGE Asking for and giving recommendations

a Look at the phrases in **bold** below. Which ones are asking for recommendations? Which are giving recommendations?

1 **Do you think** that's a good idea?
2 **If I were you, I'd** go with jewelry.
3 **It's probably worth** thinking this through a little more.
4 Well, **what would you recommend?**
5 **It's much better to** buy something that's her style.
6 **You can't go wrong** with these earrings.

b Complete the conversations with the correct form of the verbs in parentheses. Look back at the phrases in 2a to help you.

1

MICHAEL She loves books! Well, what ^{1}_____ ? (you/recommend)

VANESSA Books are great, but do you think that's enough? I mean, that sounds kind of boring. It's probably worth ^{2}_____ this through a little more. (think)

2

A Uh, she likes to play games with me sometimes, but I just don't know. What do you suggest?

B Well, if I were you, I ^{3}_____ with jewelry. A necklace, or a pair of earrings. Look, these are gorgeous. (go)

A Really? They're so … plain. I think that pair with spikes looks cooler.

B I … guess they're cool, but it's much better ^{4}_____ something that's her style. (buy)

3 CONVERSATION SKILLS
Expressing surprise

a 💬📱 Do you think Julia will like the gift Vanessa helped Michael to choose? Will she be surprised? Why / Why not?

b ▶️ 06.13 Listen to Part 2 and check your answers to 3a.

c ▶️ 06.13 Listen to Part 2 again and complete the sentences.
1 **MICHAEL** I hope you like it.
  JULIA Earrings! _____ !
2 **JULIA** Wow, these are gorgeous!
  MICHAEL _____ ? You like them?
3 **JULIA** I was sure you were just going to get me a book. And that would have been fine, but these earrings, _____ !
  MICHAEL A book? You're _____ !

d 💬📱 Take turns saying the sentences below and answering by expressing surprise.
1 I'm getting married.
2 I passed all my exams.
3 That coat costs $300.
4 I lost my phone yesterday.

4 PRONUNCIATION
Sounding interested

a ▶️ 06.14 Listen to this extract. Is the intonation flat or not? Underline the correct word in the rule.

JULIA I love them! They're exactly my style! How did you know?

> Sometimes, intonation is more important than the words we use. If we use *varied* / *flat* intonation, we may sound as if we're bored, or don't care about the subject.

b ▶️ 06.15 Listen to exchanges 1–3. Which of the B speakers sounds bored?
1 **A** I got a new job.
  B Wow. That's incredible.
2 **A** I just bought some new shoes.
  B That's amazing.
3 **A** We lost the game last night.
  B That's terrible.

c Practice saying the exchanges in 4b. Try to sound interested.

5 SPEAKING

>>> Communication 6C 💬📱 Student A: Read the instructions below. Student B: Go to p. 130.

> **Student A**
> 1 You have been offered an amazing job. The salary is very high, and it is a great opportunity. The problem is that you need to move to Berlin next month! Tell your partner your news and ask for some recommendations about what to do.
> 2 Listen to your partner's surprising news and give some recommendations.

I got an offer for a new job. It's in Berlin!

No way! That's great.

Do you think I should take it?

✅ UNIT PROGRESS TEST

→ CHECK YOUR PROGRESS

You can now do the Unit Progress Test.

6D SKILLS FOR WRITING
It's definitely worth a visit

Learn to write a review of a restaurant or café

W Positive and negative language; Adverbs

1 SPEAKING AND LISTENING

a Look at situations 1–3. Where would you go for these occasions? Choose from the locations in the box.

1 to meet friends for a chat and a cup of coffee
2 a birthday or an anniversary
3 a party at the end of the semester or the end of a language course

a café   a cheap restaurant   an expensive restaurant
a venue with music or dancing (e.g., a club)

b 💬 Compare your ideas. Do you agree?

c ▶️ 06.16 Listen to Jeff, Fabio, and Carla. Which place in photos 1–3 is each of them talking about?

d ▶️ 06.16 Listen again and answer the questions.

1 Why doesn't Jeff like the atmosphere at expensive restaurants?
2 What does he say about the food?
3 Does Fabio go to cafés alone, or with friends, or both?
4 Why does he like sidewalk cafés?
5 What does Carla do before she starts dancing?
6 What kind of music does her favorite place play?

e Think of one place to go out that you really like and one that you don't really like. Write notes about their good and bad points.

f 💬 Discuss your places. Do you agree with your partner's descriptions? Why / Why not?

2 READING

a Read the four reviews of a café on p. 77. The first reviewer gave it five stars (= excellent). How many stars do you think the other reviewers gave it?

b Read reviews a–d again. Underline any words or phrases that are used to describe the things below.

1 the atmosphere
2 the kind of food and drinks they serve
3 the quality of the food
4 the service
5 the value
6 the location

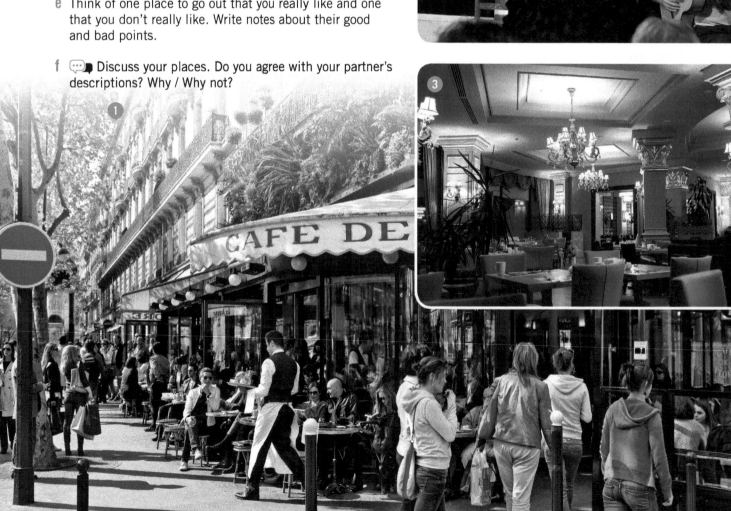

a *"Very highly recommended. Would go back again."* ★★★★★

I came here on my birthday. The coffee and cakes were delicious, and there was a relaxing atmosphere, with plenty of space. The staff were very friendly and gave us free birthday drinks. I can definitely recommend this café, and I'll be going back.

b *"Visited twice in 3 days!"* ★★★★★

We had wonderful food here. The fish was very fresh, and they had delicious salads. It's also a great place to just sit and relax. The second time we went, we just ordered coffee, and the waiters were friendly and left us alone. We stayed for three hours! It's right in the center of town, so it's a little noisy, but it's a convenient place to meet and fairly easy to get to. It's definitely worth a visit!

c *"Completely overrated."* ★★★★★

We had seen good reviews of this café, but it was extremely disappointing. The service was awful – we waited for 30 minutes before anyone even noticed we were there. We ordered pasta, but it was overcooked and the sauce was completely tasteless. My soup was tasty, but it was half cold and I had to send it back. The waiters were friendly enough, but they were so slow.

d *"A nice place to meet friends"* ★★★★★

This is a bright, friendly café, and they also serve good food, although the portions aren't very generous and it's a little overpriced. I usually go there for some coffee. It has a fairly pleasant atmosphere, and the service is always reasonably friendly and relaxed. I'd recommend it as a place to get something to drink with friends, but it might be better to eat somewhere else.

3 WRITING SKILLS Positive and negative language; Adverbs

a Add adjectives or phrases from the reviews above to the chart.

Positive	Fairly positive
delicious	friendly enough

Fairly negative	Negative
a little noisy	awful

b 💬 Compare your answers. Did you choose the same adjectives and phrases?

c Compare the two sentences. They are both negative, but they are not exactly the same. In which sentence is the writer trying not to sound too negative?

1 The portions weren't **very generous**.
2 The portions were **absolutely tiny**.

d Which of these sentences are slightly negative? Which are very negative?

1 It was extremely disappointing.
2 The bread wasn't very fresh.
3 The sauce was completely tasteless.
4 My soup wasn't really hot enough.
5 The portions were fairly small.
6 The service was awful.

e Do we use these adverbs to make adjectives or phrases stronger or weaker?

a little absolutely completely extremely fairly not really
not very slightly barely really reasonably deeply

f Change the strong comments in the sentences in 3d so that they sound weaker. Change the weaker comments so that they sound stronger.

1 It was a little disappointing.
2 The bread was really old.

4 WRITING Two reviews

a Choose two places you know (restaurants, cafés, or venues with music). Think of one place you like a lot and one place you don't really like. Write notes about the points below.

- general atmosphere
- location
- how busy it is
- what they serve
- quality of food
- service
- friendliness
- prices
- value for the money

b 💬 Compare your ideas with a partner.

c Write two reviews, one for each place.

d Work in pairs. Read your partner's reviews. Check that your partner has done the things below.

1 covered all the points in 4a
2 used appropriate adjectives and phrases
3 used adverbs appropriately

e 💬 Show your reviews to other students. Do you agree with your partner's descriptions? Why / Why not?

UNIT 6
Review and extension

1 GRAMMAR

a Read the text and <u>underline</u> the best words.

Essaouira is a wonderful place to visit. You ¹*must / should / can* enjoy walking through the streets, shopping at the market, or tasting local food. It's often windy in Essaouira, so you ²*don't have to / should / have to* bring warm clothes. The wind means that the beach isn't good for sunbathing, but you ³*ought to / shouldn't / must* go kite-surfing – it's really exciting! If you like history, you ⁴*don't have to / have to / should* explore the old part of town. There are a lot of market stalls here. If you want to buy something, discuss the price with the vendor. You certainly ⁵*shouldn't / ought to / must* pay the first price you hear!

Many people here speak English, Spanish, or French, so you ⁶*don't have to / should / must not* learn Arabic, although you ⁷*should / must / have to* probably learn a few useful phrases. You ⁸*can't / don't have to / must not* stay in expensive hotels; there are other options, including riads, which are hotels that feel like family homes.

b Complete the sentences with the correct form of the words in parentheses. Add any extra words you need.

1 A burger in my country is _____ (slightly cheap) a burger here.
2 Indonesia is _____ (a little hot) Jamaica.
3 On average, trains in Japan are _____ (much fast) trains in India.
4 Thai food is _____ (by far spicy) I've ever eaten.
5 Traveling on this subway isn't _____ (nearly expensive) traveling on the New York subway.

2 VOCABULARY

a Complete each pair of sentences with compound nouns made from the words in the boxes.

air   lot   conditioner   parking

1 There isn't a space here for the car. We'll need to find another _____ .
2 **A** It's so hot!   **B** I'll turn the _____ on.

hour   public   rush   transportation

3 Let's go at ten o'clock, when _____ is over.
4 Should we drive or use _____?

jam   light   traffic   traffic

5 Sorry I'm late. I got stuck in a _____ .
6 Wait for the _____ to change from red to green.

bike   vending   lane   machine

7 That car shouldn't be in the _____!
8 I'd like a cold drink. Is there a _____ near here?

b Complete the sentences with words for describing food.

1 I'm not hungry. Can I have something _____, like a salad?
2 I love _____ foods like chocolate and cake!
3 This hasn't been cooked properly. Look! The vegetables are still _____ .
4 This juice is really _____ . There's too much lemon in it.

3 WORDPOWER go

a Match questions 1–5 with responses a–e.

1 ☐ Where does that path **go**?
2 ☐ How did your trip **go**?
3 ☐ This is my new dress. Do these shoes **go** with it?
4 ☐ Where's the milk?
5 ☐ Was there food at the party?

a Really well. I met some very nice people.
b No, they're the wrong color.
c To the beach, I think.
d Yes, but when I got there it was all **gone**.
e It **went** bad. I threw it away.

b Match the phrases with *go* in 3a with these descriptions.

We can use:
- *go* to mean *disappear* _d_
- *go* (*with*) to mean *look similar / look good together* ____
- *go* to mean *go toward* ____
- *go* + adverb to describe how things happen (e.g., *go badly*) ____
- *go* + adjective to describe a change (e.g., *go gray*) ____

c Complete each sentence with the correct form of *go* and a word or phrase from the box, if necessary.

around   really well   with my eyes   bad

1 I had a job interview yesterday. It _____. I got the job!
2 When I turned to speak to Fred, he had already _____.
3 The road _____ the lake. It's a nice drive.
4 The store clerk said the scarf _____ .
5 Milk that is not refrigerated will eventually _____.

d 💬 Look at what the people are saying. Think of two things that each person might be talking about.

1 It went very well, thanks.

2 It went completely white.

3 It goes very well with cheese.

4 Oh, no! It's gone bad!

5 It goes over the river.

6 It's gone. Good!

⟳ REVIEW YOUR PROGRESS

How well did you do in this unit? Write 3, 2, or 1 for each objective.
3 = very well   2 = well   1 = not so well

I CAN ...	
talk about advice and rules	☐
describe food	☐
ask for and give recommendations	☐
write a review of a restaurant or café.	☐

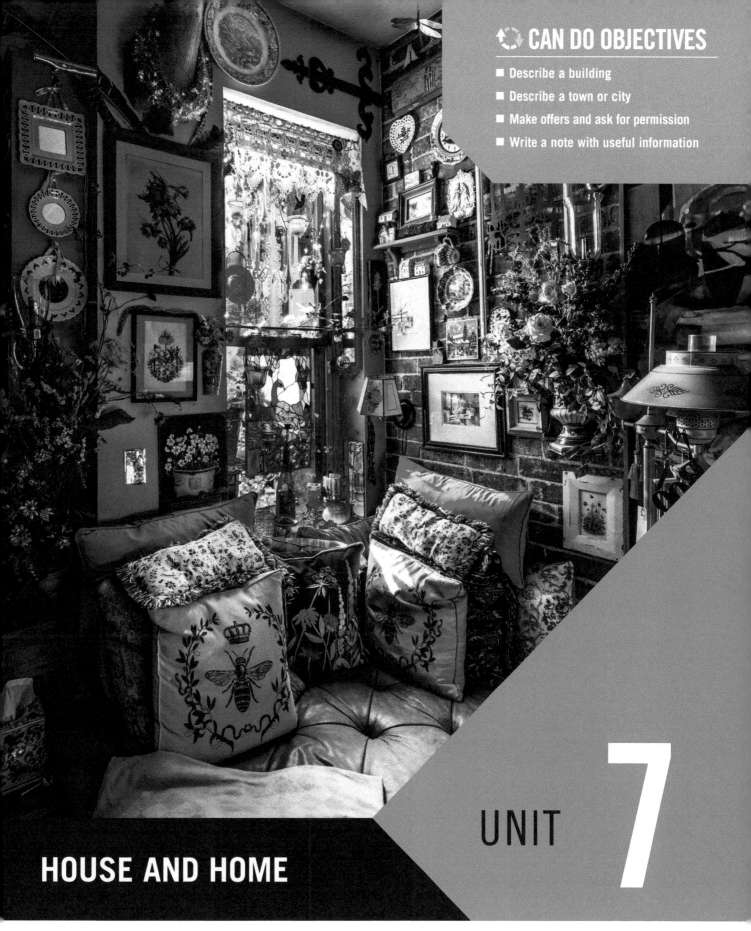

CAN DO OBJECTIVES

- Describe a building
- Describe a town or city
- Make offers and ask for permission
- Write a note with useful information

UNIT 7

HOUSE AND HOME

GETTING STARTED

a 💬 Look at the photo and answer the questions.

1 Which room in the house is this? What items can you see?
2 Would you like to have a room like this in your home? Why / Why not?
3 What is your favorite room in your home? Describe it.

b 💬 Talk about your ideal home.

1 What would it look like?
2 How big would it be?
3 Where would it be?
4 Who would live there with you?

79

7A | IT MIGHT BE A VACATION HOME

1 LISTENING

a 💬 Look at photos a–d and discuss the questions.

1 Where do you think the buildings are? Are they in the city or the country? Which country? Explain your answers.

2 Who do you think lives in each building? A large family? A young married couple? Explain your answers.

b ▶ 07.01 Listen to four people talking about photos a–d. Which photo is each person talking about?

Speaker 1 ___   Speaker 3 ___
Speaker 2 ___   Speaker 4 ___

c ▶ 07.01 Listen again. Where do the speakers think the buildings are? Who do they think lives there? Are their answers the same as yours in 1a?

d Do you like these buildings? Why / Why not?

2 GRAMMAR Modals of deduction

a Complete each sentence with one word.

1 It's very small, so it _____ belong to a big family.
2 There _____ be much space in there!
3 It _____ belong to a single person or a couple.
4 It _____ be on the outskirts of any big city.
5 It _____ not be a house.
6 Whoever lives there _____ have children.
7 Or it _____ be a vacation home.

b ▶ 07.02 Listen and check your answers.

c Match sentences 1–4 with meanings a–c. Two have the same meaning.

1 ☐ It **must** be a vacation home.
2 ☐ It **might** be a vacation home.
3 ☐ It **could** be a vacation home.
4 ☐ It **can't** be a vacation home.

a I think it's a vacation home (but I'm not sure).
b I'm sure it's a vacation home.
c I'm sure it's not a vacation home.

d Look again at the sentences in 2c. What verb form comes after *must*, *might*, *could*, and *can't*?

e ≫ Now go to Grammar Focus 7A on p. 156.

f ▶ 07.04 Pronunciation Listen to the sentences in 2c. Underline the correct word in the rule.

> When the final /t/ sound in a word is followed by a consonant sound, it is often *easier* / *harder* to hear the /t/ clearly.

g ▶ 07.05 Listen and check (✓) the sentences where you hear the final *t*. Practice saying the sentences.

1 ☐ It can't get much sun.
2 ☐ She must earn a lot of money.
3 ☐ It might be very expensive.
4 ☐ You must enjoy living here!

h 💬 Discuss the questions.

1 What do you think it might be like to live in the homes in 1a?
2 What would you see from the windows?
3 Would you have a lot of space? Are there a lot of rooms?

3 VOCABULARY Buildings

a Read the email and underline the correct words.

> ✉ 📝 ☆ 🏳 ⊗
>
> Hi James,
>
> I'm ¹*moving* / *moving my house* next Friday, so here's my new address: 82 Spring Street, Apartment 4c, Newport, Rhode Island, 02480. I'm ²*renting* / *buying* the apartment for six months, and if I like it, I'll stay longer. It's on the fourth ³*level* / *floor* of a modern apartment ⁴*building* / *landing*, and it has ⁵*views* / *sights* of the ocean!
>
> It's in a good ⁶*location* / *located*. The ⁷*neighbor* / *neighborhood* is quiet, but there are some nice cafés and stores nearby. You should come and visit. If it's sunny, we can sit on the ⁸*upstairs* / *balcony* and look at the ocean!
>
> I have to move out ⁹*of* / *to* this house on Tuesday, but I can't move ¹⁰*of* / *into* my new place until Friday, so I'll be staying with my parents for a few days next week. Are you going to be in the area?
>
> Thanks,
> Alex

b ≫ Now go to Vocabulary Focus 7A on p. 139.

4 READING

a 💬 Imagine you're going to stay for three nights in a city that you don't know. Discuss the questions.

1 What are the advantages and disadvantages of staying in:
- a hotel?
- a rented apartment?
- a spare room in a local person's house?

2 Where would you prefer to stay? Why?

b Read the introduction of "A More Personal Place to Stay" and choose the best summary.

1 How to "live like a local" on vacation
2 How to find out about a place before you visit
3 How to learn the price of accommodations

c 💬 Would you like to stay in someone else's home? What would be good or bad about it?

d Read "What the Guests Say …" and answer the questions. Write *L* (Lorena) or *K* (Kumi).

1 ☐ Who could swim at the place they stayed?
2 ☐ Who felt "at home" in the neighborhood?
3 ☐ Who could easily get around the city?
4 ☐ Who cooked their own food?
5 ☐ Who is going to see their host(s) again?

e 💬 Which of the places would you rather stay?

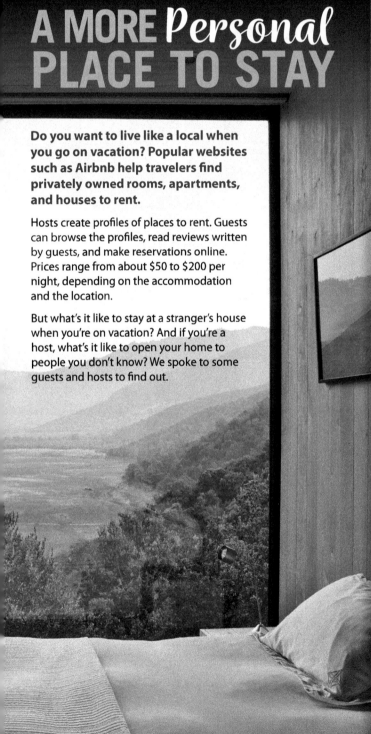

A MORE *Personal* PLACE TO STAY

Do you want to live like a local when you go on vacation? Popular websites such as Airbnb help travelers find privately owned rooms, apartments, and houses to rent.

Hosts create profiles of places to rent. Guests can browse the profiles, read reviews written by guests, and make reservations online. Prices range from about $50 to $200 per night, depending on the accommodation and the location.

But what's it like to stay at a stranger's house when you're on vacation? And if you're a host, what's it like to open your home to people you don't know? We spoke to some guests and hosts to find out.

👤 WHAT THE GUESTS SAY …

KUMI I've stayed in Berlin a few times, but I've always stayed in a hotel. This experience was completely different. I had the entire top floor of an old house, and the rent included a bicycle, too, which was great for traveling around the city. The hosts (Karl and Alexandra) were very kind, and we had good conversations at every meal. They let me use the kitchen, which was great since the restaurants nearby were very expensive. The shopkeepers in the area knew I was staying at Karl and Alexandra's, and they were all very friendly. I felt like a local by the end of the week!

LORENA My friends and I stayed in this amazing modern villa in California for ten days. It had eight bedrooms, a pool, and the biggest kitchen I've ever seen (in which Jeff, our host, cooked fantastic breakfasts for us!). Jeff was so nice. He gave us a lot of information about the local area and invited us to join him for dinner. We ended up becoming good friends – he's going to stay in my house when he comes to Ecuador next year.

f 💬 What do you think are the advantages and disadvantages of being an Airbnb host?

g Read "What the Hosts Say ... ." Do they mention the advantages and disadvantages you talked about?

🏠 WHAT THE HOSTS SAY ...

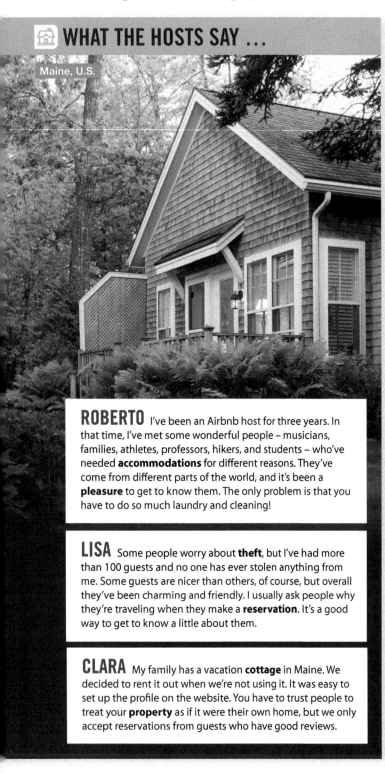

Maine, U.S.

ROBERTO I've been an Airbnb host for three years. In that time, I've met some wonderful people – musicians, families, athletes, professors, hikers, and students – who've needed **accommodations** for different reasons. They've come from different parts of the world, and it's been a **pleasure** to get to know them. The only problem is that you have to do so much laundry and cleaning!

LISA Some people worry about **theft**, but I've had more than 100 guests and no one has ever stolen anything from me. Some guests are nicer than others, of course, but overall they've been charming and friendly. I usually ask people why they're traveling when they make a **reservation**. It's a good way to get to know a little about them.

CLARA My family has a vacation **cottage** in Maine. We decided to rent it out when we're not using it. It was easy to set up the profile on the website. You have to trust people to treat your **property** as if it were their own home, but we only accept reservations from guests who have good reviews.

h Read the texts above again and match the words in **bold** with the definitions.

1 a building that someone owns
2 place(s) to stay
3 a small house in the country
4 an enjoyable experience
5 the crime of stealing something
6 an arrangement to stay somewhere (e.g., a hotel room)

5 SPEAKING

a 💬 Look at the buildings below and discuss the questions.
1 How old is each building?
2 What do you think it's like inside?
3 Would you like to live there?

b 💬 Imagine you are going on vacation with your partner. Discuss which of the houses/apartments you would like to s[*] in. Can you agree on one house/apartment to visit?

> I'd like to stay in the apartment in photo e. New York must be a really great city to visit.

a
Cappadocia, Turkey

b
Amsterdam, The Netherlands

c
Essex, U.K.

d
Cork, Ireland

f
Miami, U.S.

e
New York City, U.S.

7B THERE ARE PLENTY OF THINGS TO DO

Learn to describe a town or city

- **G** Quantifiers
- **V** Verbs and prepositions

1 LISTENING

a 💬 Where did you grow up – in a big city or a small town? What was good and bad about it?

b Read "Five Reasons Why Small Towns Are Better Than Cities." Do you agree with the reasons in the list? Can you add any more reasons?

c 💬 Think of five reasons why cities are better places to live than small towns. Tell a partner.

d ▶ 07.08 Listen to Tim and Kate's conversation. Are Tim's reasons the same as yours in 1c?

e ▶ 07.08 Listen again. Are these statements true (T) or false (F)?

1 Kate grew up in a small town.
2 Tim wouldn't want to live in a small town.
3 Kate thinks small towns are safer.
4 More people have car accidents in the city than in the country.
5 People who live in the country have a smaller carbon footprint.

f 💬 Discuss the questions.

1 Where do you think it's safer to live – in the city or in the country? Think about:
   - driving • crime • hospitals • other ideas
2 Is your (nearest) city designed in a way that's good for the environment? Why / Why not?
3 How could your (nearest) city be better? Think about:
   - public transportation • bike lanes • other ideas

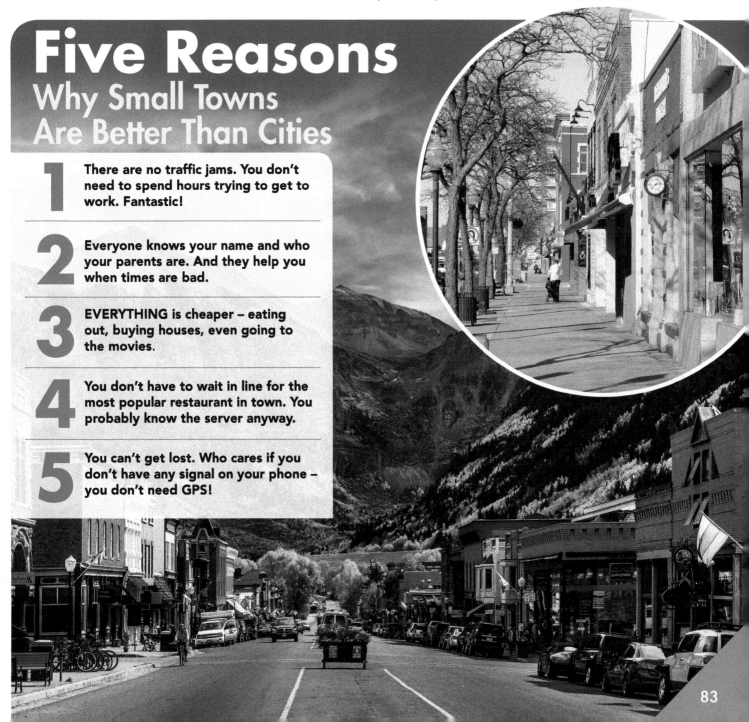

Five Reasons
Why Small Towns Are Better Than Cities

1 There are no traffic jams. You don't need to spend hours trying to get to work. Fantastic!

2 Everyone knows your name and who your parents are. And they help you when times are bad.

3 EVERYTHING is cheaper – eating out, buying houses, even going to the movies.

4 You don't have to wait in line for the most popular restaurant in town. You probably know the server anyway.

5 You can't get lost. Who cares if you don't have any signal on your phone – you don't need GPS!

2 VOCABULARY Verbs and prepositions

a Complete the sentences with the words in the box.

about (x2)   on   to

1 People care _____ you.
2 It's like you belong _____ one big family.
3 That makes sense if you think _____ it.
4 You can't rely _____ public transportation in the country like you can in the city.

b ▶07.09 **Pronunciation** Listen and check your answers to 2a. Then complete the rule.

When we use a verb and a preposition, we *usually / don't usually* stress the verb and *stress / don't stress* the preposition.

c ▶07.09 Listen again and practice saying the sentences.

d Match the verbs in the box with the prepositions. Use some verbs more than once.

apologize   argue   believe   belong   care
complain   cope   depend   ~~pay~~   ~~rely~~
succeed   ~~think~~   ~~wait~~   worry

1 _____ - - - - - with someone
2 _____ - - - - - with something
think
3 _____
4 _____ - - - - about something
5 _____
pay
wait - - - - for something
6 _____
7 _____
8 _____ - - - - in something
in doing something
rely
on someone/something
9 _____
10 _____
11 _____ to someone
12 _____

e Complete each sentence with the correct form of a verb + preposition from 2d.

1 Do I like living in the country? That _____ _____ the weather – when it's warm and sunny, I love it!
2 My friend just moved from the country to the city, and she's finding it hard to _____ _____ all the noise.
3 He moved here to look for work, but he hasn't _____ _____ finding a job yet, unfortunately.
4 I'd like to _____ _____ what I said earlier. I didn't mean to be so rude.
5 I _____ _____ the parking attendant about the fine for ten minutes, but in the end I had to pay it.
6 People _____ _____ the traffic here, but it isn't bad compared to a big city.
7 **A** Do you _____ _____ bad luck?
  B No, not really. I think people are in control of their own lives.
8 All of the land near the river is private – it _____ _____ the university. You can't walk there.

f 💬 Complete the game instructions below with the correct prepositions. Then play the game in teams.

"**TWO**" Think of two things for each category. You win a point for each answer that no other team has written.

a ways you can pay _for_ things
  1 _____   2 _____
b things hotel guests often complain _____
  1 _____   2 _____
c ways you can apologize _____ being late
  1 _____   2 _____
d things people often do when they're waiting _____ a bus or train
  1 _____   2 _____
e things that a lot of adults worry _____
  1 _____   2 _____
f things that a lot of children believe _____
  1 _____   2 _____

3 GRAMMAR Quantifiers

a 💬 Discuss the questions.
   1 Are there parks and other green spaces where you live?
   2 What activities can people do there?
   3 How often do you use parks and other green spaces?

b Look at the large photo of the High Line park. What's unusual about this park? Read "The High Line, New York City" and check.

c Read the article again. Underline the correct words.
   1 There are *a lot of / enough* species of plants in the High Line park.
   2 How *much / many* visitors go to the park each year?
   3 There is *very little / too much* crime in the park.
   4 Jen thinks there are *very few / too many* tourists there.
   5 The website contains *a lot of / not enough* information.
   6 There's *not much / too much* trash in the park.

The High Line, NEW YORK CITY

Even the most enthusiastic city lover needs green space from time to time. In New York, one of the best places to find some nature is the High Line. Originally a 1930s railway bridge, this park opened in 2006 – ten meters above the street! It has more than 200 species of plants and spectacular views of the Hudson River. The park now attracts 4 million visitors a year, who escape the city streets to take a walk, take photos, and even get something to eat at one of the cafés. The High Line website (www.thehighline.org) is full of information about the history of the park and how they built it.

What the locals say

I love the High Line. It's calm and beautiful. It's safe, too – apparently the crime rate is very low.
Pablo

It used to be a nice, quiet place to go. Now it's full of tourists. Don't go on weekends! But one good thing is that it's very clean – they pick up all the trash regularly.
Jen

Make sure that you allow plenty of time. You need about three hours to see it all. There's a lot to see – and you don't want to miss any of it!
Kira

d ≫ Now go to Grammar Focus 7B on p. 156.

e Write sentences about each of the places below. Use quantifiers and the words in the box, and your own ideas. Don't include the name of the place.
   • a city area that you know
   • a country area that you know

| noise | crime | space | people | flowers | things to do |
| stores | cafés | wildlife | views | pollution | traffic |

It's a great place. There isn't much traffic, and there's very little pollution.

f 💬 Read your sentences aloud. Can your partner guess where the places are?

> A lot of people go there on weekends, but there's enough space for everyone. There aren't many stores or cafés.

> Is it the beach?

4 SPEAKING

a You are going to talk about the area where you live. Write notes about these questions:
   • Is it a healthy or safe place to live? Why / Why not?
   • What do people like about it? (e.g., parks, restaurants)
   • What do people complain about? (e.g., the noise, the roads)

b 💬 Take turns talking about your areas. Would the places you talk about be good to live in for each of the people below? Why / Why not?
   • a teenager who likes movies and music
   • a family with young children
   • an elderly couple
   • someone who likes sports and outdoor activities

EVERYDAY ENGLISH
Is there anything we can do to help?

Learn to make offers and ask for permission

- P Sounding polite
- S Imagining how people feel

1 LISTENING

a 💬 Discuss the questions.

1 Do you take a gift when you visit someone's home? What might you bring?
2 What should you do to be polite when visiting someone's home? (e.g., arrive on time, take your shoes off, etc.)

b 💬 Bradley is going to spend his vacation with his friend Fausto at Fausto's parents' house. How do you think Bradley might feel? What kind of gift might he bring?

c ▶️ 07.14 Listen to Part 1 and check your ideas.

d ▶️ 07.14 Listen again. Are the sentences true (T) or false (F)?

1 Bradley hasn't met Fausto's parents before.
2 Fausto's mother's favorite flowers are tulips.
3 Alicia needs to check on the food.
4 David is an accountant.
5 Fausto says he told his parents Bradley was a vegetarian.

e Do you think that Bradley has been a good guest? Has he made a good first impression?

2 USEFUL LANGUAGE Offers, requests, and asking for permission

a Match questions 1–5 with responses a–e.

1 **Is there anything we can do to help**? — ☐ c
2 **Do you think you could** give me a hand in here? — ☐
3 Come in and **have a** seat, Bradley. — ☐
4 **Would you excuse me** for a moment? — ☐
5 **Let me** make you a salad or something. — ☐

a Of course.
b Sure.
c Oh no, it's all under control!
d A salad would be great. Thanks.
e Oh, thank you.

b ▶️ 07.15 Listen and check your answers.

c What phrases in **bold** in 2a do we use to ...

1 offer something politely?   3 ask for permission?
2 ask for help politely?

d Match requests 1–5 with responses a–e.

1 ☐ Do you mind if I borrow some money?
2 ☐ May I sit here?
3 ☐ Do you think I could have a glass of water?
4 ☐ Can I use your phone for a moment?
5 ☐ Would you mind if I opened the window?

a Yes, of course. Let me get you one.
b Not at all. How much do you want?
c Sure. Here it is.
d Not at all. It's hot in here.
e Of course. There's plenty of space.

3 LISTENING

a 💬🔊 How do you think Bradley feels about meeting Fausto's parents for the first time?

b ▶️07.16 Listen to Part 2 and check your ideas.

c ▶️07.16 Listen again. Are the sentences true (T) or false (F)?

1 Fausto thinks Bradley made a bad first impression.
2 Bradley is going to stay in a hotel.

4 CONVERSATION SKILLS
Imagining how people feel

a ▶️07.17 Complete the sentences with the missing words. Listen and check.

1 You _____ excited about the soccer game this afternoon.
2 I _____ that's very interesting.

b Read the exchanges and underline the phrases we use to imagine what someone else is feeling.

1 **A** I have three part-time jobs at the moment.
  B You must be very tired!
2 **A** I have an important interview tomorrow.
  B I expect you're a little nervous!

c 💬🔊 Look at the sentences below. Respond with *must be* and an appropriate adjective.

1 I'm planning a vacation to France.
2 I just broke my tooth!
3 I lost my smartphone – and I can't remember any of my friends' numbers.
4 I'm learning Japanese at the moment.

> I'm planning a vacation to France.

> That must be exciting!

d 💬🔊 Tell your partner about some of the things below. Answer with a phrase from 4a or 4b.

- something you're planning on doing soon
- a hobby you have
- a problem you have at school/work

> I have Spanish lessons at 7:30 in the morning, before I go to work.

> That must be tiring.

> Yes, but I really enjoy them.

5 PRONUNCIATION Sounding polite

a ▶️07.18 Listen to these sentences spoken twice. Which sentence sounds more polite, a or b?

1 Fausto, do you think you could give me a hand in here? *a / b*
2 Hello! It's great to meet you, Bradley. *a / b*

b ▶️07.19 Listen to three more pairs of sentences. Which sentences sound more polite, a or b?

1 How long are you staying? *a / b*
2 She seems really great. *a / b*
3 I'm really happy to hear that. *a / b*

c 💬 Practice saying the sentences in 5b with polite intonation.

6 SPEAKING

≫ Communication 7C 💬 Student A: Read the instructions below. Student B: Go to p. 132.

Student A

1 You are staying with Student B in their home. During the conversation, ask permission to:
  - use the Internet
  - take a shower
  - wash some clothes

2 Student B is a new coworker in your office. Ask them how it's going and try to sound interested (e.g., *That must be …*). They will ask you for permission to do things. Decide whether or not to give permission.

✅ UNIT PROGRESS TEST

→ CHECK YOUR PROGRESS

You can now do the Unit Progress Test.

1 SPEAKING

a 💬 Talk about a recent vacation.

1 What kinds of activities did you do?
2 Did the people you were with want to do the same things as you or different things?
3 Think of a vacation you would like to go on. What would you do on the vacation?

2 READING AND LISTENING

a 💬 You're going to read about vacationing in Miami. Before you do, discuss the questions.

1 Where is Miami? Have you ever been there? Do you know anyone who's been there?
2 What is it like, or what do you imagine it's like? Talk about the points below.
   - the weather
   - the people
   - the buildings
   - the atmosphere
   - things to see and do

b 💬 Read about the top five things to do in and around Miami. Which things would you like to do? Why? Are there any things you would *not* want to do? Why not?

c ▶ 07.20 Rossana is talking to a coworker. Listen to their conversation and answer the questions.

1 How many people are in Rossana's family?
2 Where are they staying?
3 Which of the "top five things" are they going to do?

d ▶ 07.20 Listen again and write notes in the chart.

	Where do they want to go?	Why do they want to go there?
Rossana's daughter		
Rossana's son		
Rossana's husband		
Rossana		

e 💬 Do you think Rossana is looking forward to the vacation? Why / Why not?

TOP FIVE THINGS TO DO
... in and around Miami, Florida

1 Admire the architecture of Miami Beach
Wander the streets of Miami Beach and admire the art deco hotels and houses from the 1930s. The movie stars from the 1930s stayed here when they came to Miami. Many of the buildings have been repainted in their original colors.

2 Go to the beach
Miami has endless sandy beaches along the coast. You can find crowds if you want them, or you can have a beach to yourself. And the water is always warm.

3 Visit the Everglades
Ninety minutes from Miami are the Everglades, a huge area of natural swamp that is home to alligators, snakes, and rare birds. Take a boat through the area and get a close-up view of the wildlife.

4 Spend a day at Walt Disney World
Walt Disney World is not very far from Miami – a great day trip. You can find all the characters from Disney movies and have hours of fun with (or without) your kids.

5 Take a trip to Cape Canaveral
North of Miami is Cape Canaveral, where the United States sends some of its rockets into space. You can tour the Kennedy Space Center and see where they built the Apollo rockets that went to the moon.

3 READING

a Read the note below that Rossana's cousin left in the apartment in Miami. <u>Underline</u> the correct words.

1 The streets are safe *during the day / all the time*.
2 The apartment is *in downtown / just outside* Miami.
3 The apartment is *right next to / far from* the ocean.
4 Alvaro will be away for *a week / more than a week*.

b Which adjectives in the box best describe the tone of the note? Which words or phrases in the note helped you decide?

> friendly   formal   funny   practical

c Match the purposes a–f with sections 1–6 of the note.

a ☐ to explain options for buying food
b ☐ to give information about going to places farther away
c ☐ to finish the note
d ☐ to greet the reader and say what the note is about
e ☐ to give safety advice about the area around the apartment
f ☐ to give information about things in the apartment

d What general order are the sections in? Choose the correct answer.

1 things they need to know now → things they need to know later
2 things that are very important → things that are less important
3 things that are less important → things that are more important

① Welcome to Miami! Hope you have a nice stay in the apartment. Here are a few things you need to know …

② Please make yourselves at home and help yourselves to anything in the kitchen. There's some chicken in the fridge and a lot of fruit and salad, so that should be enough for a couple of meals. I also got a couple of pizzas for the kids – they're in the freezer.

③ After that, you'll need to go shopping. The best place is the Sunshine Center. Go out of the main entrance of the apartment and turn left, and you'll see it about 100 meters down the road. It has a couple of supermarkets, a good bookstore, and a few good places to eat. Otherwise, there's a good place for burgers a little farther down the road. Apart from that, there are some good restaurants by the ocean, but they're a little farther away.

④ By the way, if you do go out in the evening, don't walk around late at night – the streets around here are not very safe at night, although they're OK during the day.

⑤ Anyway, the car's in the parking lot, so you can use that for any trips. If you're going into Miami, another possibility is to take the train, but you'll find the car easier! You'll also need the car to go to the beach. The nearest one is Golden Beach, about a 15-minute drive away. Another option is Ocean Beach, about 30 minutes farther north, which is usually much less crowded. Alternatively, you could try Miami Beach, but it can be difficult to park there.

⑥ Enjoy your stay and see you in two weeks!
Love,
Alvaro

4 WRITING SKILLS Offering choices

a What do the words in **bold** below mean?

1 The Sunshine Center has a few good places to eat. **Otherwise**, there's a good place for burgers a little farther down the road.
   a if you don't like that idea
   b however
   c finally

2 The nearest one is Golden Beach, about a 15-minute drive away. **Another option is** Ocean Beach, about 30 minutes farther north.
   a a different direction is
   b a different choice is
   c a much better beach is

b Read the note again and find three more words or phrases that you could use instead of *Otherwise* or *Another option is …* .

c Use words or phrases from 4a and 4b in the second sentences below.

1 If you drive north, you can visit Walt Disney World. You can also go to the Space Center at Cape Canaveral.
   Another option is the Space Center at Cape Canaveral.

2 There are a lot of good restaurants in Miami Beach. Or you can try the restaurants in South Beach.

3 You can get an inter-city bus to go to the West Coast. You can also rent a car for a few days.

4 You can drive through the Everglades to look at the birds and alligators. You can also see them by boat.

5 WRITING A note with useful information

a You are going to write a note for someone who will be staying in your home while you are away. Think about:

- things in the house/apartment
- things they can and can't do
- things you want to ask them to do
- food and shopping
- things to do in the area.

b 💬 Compare your ideas with a partner.

c Read another student's note and answer the questions.

1 Did you understand all the information?
2 Did they put the information in a logical order?
3 Did they use words and phrases from 4a or 4b correctly?

UNIT 7
Review and extension

1 GRAMMAR

a Underline the correct answer.

1 There are *a lot / too many / too much* stairs in this building!
2 There isn't *enough light / light enough / enough of light*. It's always dark.
3 There's too *many / few / much* noise outside.
4 It has *a lot / a lot of / much* windows.
5 There are very *little / much / few* buildings in the area.
6 It doesn't have *many / much / little* floors.

b 💬 Discuss the pictures. Use *must*, *might*, *could*, and *can't*.

1 What kind of person are they?
2 How old are they?
3 Where are they?

(a)

(b)

2 VOCABULARY

a Complete the text with the words in the box.

building   floor   location   neighborhood   views

Vacation Home Swap

This summer, we exchanged homes with the Acuna family from Lisbon. Our home is in a quiet ¹_____ in western Vermont, with beautiful ²_____ of Lake Champlain. The Acunas live on the third ³_____ of an apartment ⁴_____ in the Portuguese capital. The apartment is in a lively ⁵_____, and there are a lot of places to visit nearby. Home swapping is a fantastic way to discover new places.

b Complete each sentence with a preposition.

1 Don't worry _____ the neighbors.
2 Who does that house belong _____?
3 You'll have to wait a long time _____ a bus.
4 How do you cope _____ the cold winters here?
5 You can't rely _____ public transportation here.
6 We succeeded _____ finding a good hotel.
7 Are you going to complain _____ the noise?

3 WORDPOWER *over*

a Match questions 1–5 with responses a–e.

1 ☐ When did you paint the house?
2 ☐ How many people live in Hong Kong?
3 ☐ How long was the meeting?
4 ☐ Can we start the test?
5 ☐ What's the matter?

a **Over** the summer.
b Yes, turn your papers **over** and begin.
c **Over** 7 million.
d You're getting mud all **over** the floor!
e It started at 2:00, and it was **over** by 3:15.

b Match the meanings of *over* with sentences a–e in 3a.

1 ☐ finished
2 ☐ more than
3 ☐ during (a period of time)
4 ☐ the other side up
5 ☐ covering

c Complete each sentence with *over* and the words in the box. One sentence only needs *over*.

16   a lifetime   the last few days
the next few days   the world

1 What businesses from your country are known all _____?
2 How much work have you done _____?
3 What can you do in your country when you are _____? How about 18?
4 What kinds of things do people learn _____?
5 When was the last time you were sad that something was _____?
6 What are you going to do _____?

d 💬 Ask and answer the questions in 3c.

⟳ REVIEW YOUR PROGRESS

How well did you do in this unit? Write 3, 2, or 1 for each objective.
3 = very well   2 = well   1 = not so well

I CAN ...	
describe a building	☐
describe a town or city	☐
make offers and ask for permission	☐
write a note with useful information.	☐

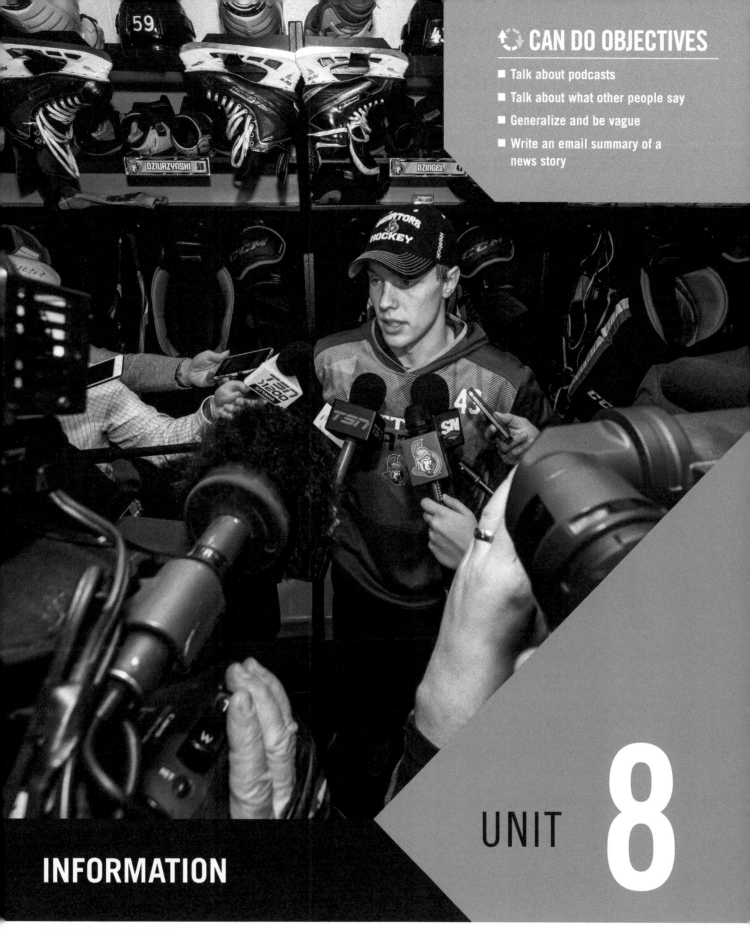

CAN DO OBJECTIVES

- Talk about podcasts
- Talk about what other people say
- Generalize and be vague
- Write an email summary of a news story

INFORMATION

UNIT **8**

GETTING STARTED

a 💬 Ask and answer the questions.

1 What is happening in the photo?
2 What do you think happened before the photo was taken?
3 What might happen next?
4 What would be a good caption for this photo if it appeared in a newspaper or online?

b 💬 Talk about an interesting story you heard recently. Where did you hear it (e.g., in the news, on a podcast, on social media)? Ask and answer questions to find out more about each other's stories.

8A | I REPLIED THAT I'D BEEN BORED WITH MY MUSIC

1 SPEAKING AND VOCABULARY
Sharing information

a 💬 Discuss the questions.

1 What do you think is the best way to share information with friends and family? Why?
2 If you had to send out important information at school, at work, or in the community, how would you do this? What are the benefits of that method?
3 Do you ever want to share ideas and opinions with others? What's the best way to do this?

b Complete the sentences with the correct form of the verbs in the box.

deliver	create	send	put up	hold	post	brainstorm

1 I _____ a text to Monica and told her to come ten minutes earlier if she could.
2 I only _____ on social media if I do something interesting, like going on vacation.
3 The best way to advertise the book sale is to _____ posters all around the campus.
4 She loves local history so much that she has decided to _____ a podcast series about it.
5 When I was younger, I used to _____ newspapers on my bike.
6 Before we write our essays, we should all _____ ideas together as a group.
7 Last week, the city council _____ a meeting to get feedback on the new bike lanes.

c 💬 Look at the verb phrases in 1b. Have you done any of these things recently? Tell your partner.

d ≫ Now go to Vocabulary Focus 8A on p. 140.

2 READING

a 💬 Discuss the questions.

1 Do you ever listen to podcasts? How often? Where?
2 Why do you think podcasts have become popular?
3 How easy or difficult do you think it is to make a podcast? Explain your answer.

b 💬 Read the article about making podcasts. In your opinion, does it sound easy or difficult? Why?

Thinking of Making a Podcast?
JUST GIVE IT A TRY!

Not so very long ago, people got their news from the radio, their entertainment from television, and their knowledge from books. But, in case you hadn't noticed, times are changing. These days people can get all of that from one source: podcasts.

More than half of all Americans say they have listened to at least one podcast in their life, and many of us just can't get enough of them. They are fun and they are informative, but most of all, they are portable. Our favorite places to listen are at home, in the car, or on public transportation. Podcasts are perfect for taking the pain out of long traffic jams or boring trips to work on the subway!

Not only are a lot of people listening to podcasts, but a lot of people are now also making them. In some ways, they are very easy to make. Anyone can do it – all you need is a microphone and a computer. However, making a podcast that people really want to listen to is a little more challenging. You need to think about what's going to make people listen – what's going to get their attention? And more importantly, what's going to make them tune in again … and again … and again?

The best way to learn to make a podcast is to just do it. You'll learn a lot by just giving it a try. The following are some useful tips to guide you in the process.

c Read the article again and write notes on the following topics.

1 podcast listening in the U.S. _____
2 places where people listen _____
3 basic requirements to make a podcast _____
4 building your number of listeners _____
5 making sure your content is good _____
6 talking on a podcast _____
7 before uploading _____
8 after you've uploaded _____

d Find expressions in the article that match these meanings. The first example is done for you:

1 make other people notice you *get their attention*
2 try to do something _____
3 pleased or satisfied with something _____
4 do what you say you will do _____
5 learned from doing something _____

3 LISTENING

a 💬 What are the best and worst places to listen to podcasts? Why?

b ▶ 08.01 Listen to Andrea. She is being interviewed on a podcast about podcasts. Answer the questions.

1 How did she start listening to podcasts?
2 What different types of podcasts does she listen to?

CONTENT

Before you grab a microphone and start talking, think about what you want to say. Your podcast series should have an overall aim or purpose, and each episode should feel like it's taking your listeners somewhere. It helps to think of your podcast as a kind of journey. You will probably need to plan what you say – not many people are great at improvising.

RECORDING and EDITING

If you record yourself on your podcast, try to sound as natural as possible. Don't use a special voice – just imagine you're talking to your friends. If your podcast isn't trying to be serious, make it sound like you're enjoying yourself. Finding and inviting interesting guests on your podcast can really help. You will probably record more material than you want to upload. This means you should edit it and only use what's relevant and interesting.

UPLOADING

Once you're happy with your episode, all you need to do is upload it. But don't imagine that thousands of people are going to find and listen to what you have to say. Use social media to tell people about your podcast, and be realistic about how many listeners you can expect to attract when you are starting out. It takes time to build an audience – and it's important to treat your audience with respect and deliver on your promises. If you say you're going to produce one episode a week, make sure you do that. And if you're running late one week, let your listeners know.

Podcasts are fun to do. If yours doesn't end up being a big hit, it doesn't matter. You might lose some of your time, but you will have gained from the experience. So what are you waiting for? Get out there and give it a try!

c ▶ 08.01 Listen again. Are the following sentences true (T) or false (F)? Correct the false sentences.

1 She first listened to podcasts at home and used her computer.
2 She found it hard not to laugh at the comedy podcast on the train.
3 Listening to the comedy podcast made the trip to work take longer.
4 The first podcast she listens to each day is the news.
5 On the train she always listens to a comedy podcast.
6 From podcasts, she has picked up a lot of ideas about baking cakes.
7 She really enjoys crime serial podcasts.
8 She's found out useful information for her job from podcasts.

d ▶ 08.02 Pronunciation Listen to the words below from the podcast. How are the letters *c*, *g*, and *k* in bold pronounced?

pod**c**ast a**g**o **g**uess **c**ommute wor**k**
giving **c**oncentrate ba**k**ing **g**ood or**g**anization

e Complete the rules with /g/ or /k/.

1 When we say _____, there is a sound in the throat.
2 When we say _____, there is no sound in the throat.

f ▶ 08.02 Listen again and repeat the words.

g 💬 If people listen to music or podcasts on public transportation, they can't hear what's going on around them. What kinds of problems can this cause?

4 GRAMMAR Reported speech (statements and questions)

a Andrea wrote an email to a friend about some of the things she said in the interview. Read the message and underline any reported speech.

✉ ✏ ☆ ⚑ ⊗

Hi Sandy,

The interview went well. First, the interviewer asked me how I had started listening to podcasts. I replied that I'd been bored with all my music and had checked out the available podcasts on my way to the subway station. Then we talked about my podcast listening habits. I said that each day, as I was walking to the subway, I listened to a news podcast. And then I mentioned all the different kinds of podcasts I listen to. He asked me if I listened to podcast series. I told him that I loved them. I also said that podcasts could be useful for my job. I told him that I'd worked for a charity organization for the past four years, and I'd picked up some really helpful ideas by listening to podcasts.

See you soon,
Andrea

b What did Andrea and the interviewer actually say? Complete the sentences in direct speech.

1 Interviewer: "How _____ you _____ listening to podcasts?"
2 "I _____ bored with all my music, so I _____ out the available podcasts on my way to the subway station," replied Andrea.
3 "Each day, as I _____ to the subway station, I _____ to a news podcast," said Andrea.
4 Interviewer: "_____ you _____ to any podcast series?"
5 "I _____ them," Andrea replied.
6 "Podcasts _____ useful for my job," Andrea told the interviewer.
7 "I _____ for a charity organization for the past four years. I _____ some really helpful ideas by listening to podcasts," said Andrea.

c ▶ 08.03 Listen and check your answers.

d Underline the correct words in the rules.

1 When we report what someone has said or written, we often change the tense of the direct speech *backward / forward* in time.
2 We use *question word order / normal word order* in reported questions.
3 We often don't change the tense when we report things that are *still true / no longer true*.

e Write the tense we use for reported speech.

Direct speech	Reported speech
simple present	_____
simple past	_____
present continuous	_____
present perfect	_____
can	_____

f ≫ Now go to Grammar Focus 8A on p. 158.

g Work in pairs. Write a story using reported speech and questions.

1 Write the first two sentences. Begin like this and continue using reported speech:
   My friend called me a few weeks ago with some news. He/She said ...
2 Pass your sentences to another pair. Read the sentences you received and add another sentence. Begin:
   I asked him/her ...
3 Pass your sentences to another pair. Read the sentences you received and add another sentence. Begin:
   He/She said ...
4 Pass your sentences to another pair. Read the sentences and add a final sentence.

h 💬 Check that the reported speech is correct. Then read your story to the class.

5 SPEAKING

a 💬 Work with a partner. Look at the opinions about podcasts. Do you agree with them? Why / Why not?

1 Podcasts have completely changed the way we share information. They're a useful way to show people a different point of view.
2 Podcasts are a very valuable tool in education because you can learn so much from them.
3 On podcasts, you just have ordinary people saying anything they like. Some of the opinions they express are too strong.
4 Podcasts just feed people more and more information and stop them from thinking for themselves.
5 Podcasts are a fantastic form of entertainment that you can take with you almost anywhere.

b 💬 Work in small groups and discuss the opinions.

1 SPEAKING AND READING

a 💬 Discuss the questions.

1 Do you read online reviews for any of these things?
- restaurants, cafés, or clubs
- places to go on vacation
- things to buy (e.g., computers, movies, phones, cars)

2 How much do you trust online reviews? Explain your answer.

b 💬 Read the review of The Shed at Dulwich and look at the photo. What is the reviewer's opinion of the restaurant? Would you like to eat there? Why / Why not?

c 💬 Now read "The Restaurant That Wasn't There" and look at the photos on p. 131. How is the restaurant different from the review?

The Shed at Dulwich ★★★★★
Reviewed May 16

If you enjoy creative, exciting food, then you'll love The Shed! My husband and I occasionally take a trip to London from our home in the country. We both love food, and we love to try new places. We came across The Shed at Dulwich on the Internet. They don't take reservations online, so I had to call. It took over a week of calling to get through to them and finally reserve a table, but we weren't disappointed. The whole experience was wonderful. The portions were pretty small, but the food was perfectly cooked and our server made us feel really special. All their food is organic and comes from their own gardens, so the menu changes according to the season – a wonderful idea! We'll certainly go back!

The Restaurant That Wasn't There

Have you ever been fooled by fake reviews online? Have you gone to a restaurant with five-star reviews only to find the food was terrible when you got there? And have you ever wished you could do something about it? Well, that's what London journalist Oobah Butler did. He managed to make his own garden shed into a five-star-rated restaurant, complete with a fake website and fake reviews.

Butler had always been concerned that online restaurant reviews might not always be genuine and that some of the people who wrote them had never actually eaten in the places they reviewed. Then one day in April, while sitting in his garden shed at home, he had an idea: if people were happy to believe anything they read online, maybe it would be possible not just to fake a restaurant review but to fake a restaurant itself. So he set out to turn his garden shed into a top-rated London restaurant.

He created a website for The Shed at Dulwich, gave his street as the address (but no house number), and called it a "reservation-only restaurant." Then he made up an attractive menu with each dish named after a particular feeling – Love, Happy, Comfort, and so on. He also took photos of the dishes, using things he found around the house – a kitchen sponge covered in coffee grounds, dishwasher tablets, and shaving cream – all beautifully arranged on plates to look like expensive dishes. And then he submitted his restaurant to online review sites and waited.

Setting up the website was easy, but becoming well known was going to be a little more difficult. He started out ranked at 18,149, so he needed some convincing reviews, and these needed to be written by real people in different places to avoid the anti-scam technology used by review websites. So he contacted all his friends and acquaintances and asked them to write reviews.

To his surprise, a few weeks later people started calling to make reservations. As the restaurant didn't exist, he had to reply that they were fully booked for weeks in advance, and this made the restaurant appear even more popular. Over the next month, the phone kept ringing, and he also had inquiries from people who were interested in working at The Shed and from companies who wanted to send him free samples of products.

Six months later, The Shed was ranked number 30 online out of all London restaurants, and he was receiving inquiries by phone and email from all over the world. Then in November, he found out that The Shed was London's top-rated restaurant.

He wasn't sure what to do next, but at this point he felt that it wasn't worth pretending any longer. So he decided to make his shed into a real restaurant. He put out a few chairs and tables and held an opening party for selected guests, serving microwaved meals bought from a local supermarket. The guests seemed to enjoy eating their microwaved food, and one couple even asked if they could come again.

So perhaps they really did think it was the best restaurant in London!

d Read the article again and write notes in answer to these questions.

1 What gave Oobah Butler the idea?
2 How did he keep the location secret?
3 How did he get positive reviews?
4 What was unusual about the menu?
5 How did he create the dishes pictured on the website?
6 At what point did he open the restaurant?
7 What kind of food did he serve?

e 💬🔊 What do you think about this story? Decide which comment(s) you agree with. Explain your answer(s).

1 This shows that online reviews are a waste of time.
2 It's easy to deceive people online, so you should be careful what you read.
3 What Oobah Butler did was wrong, and he should feel bad about it.
4 Some people waste a lot of money on things just because they are fashionable.

2 GRAMMAR Verb patterns

a Match the verb patterns in sentences 1–4 with rules a–d.

1 **Setting up** the website was easy.
2 At this point he felt that it wasn't worth **pretending** any longer.
3 The guests seemed to enjoy **eating** their microwaved food.
4 He also had inquiries from people who were interested in **working** at The Shed.

We use verb + -ing:
a after prepositions
b after certain verbs (e.g., *keep*, *start*, *love*)
c after some expressions (e.g., *it's worth*, *it's no use*)
d as the subject of a sentence

b Match the verb patterns in sentences 1–4 with rules a–d.

1 People are happy **to believe** anything they read online.
2 Oobah Butler managed **to make** his garden shed into a five-star-rated restaurant.
3 They needed to be written by real people in different places **to avoid** anti-scam technology.
4 He wasn't sure what **to do** next.

We use an infinitive:
a after question words
b after certain verbs (e.g., *want*, *plan*, *seem*, *decide*)
c after certain adjectives (e.g., *difficult*, *good*, *important*)
d to show purpose

c ≫ Now go to Grammar Focus 8B on p. 158.

d Write the correct form of the verbs in parentheses. Then choose an ending or add your own idea to make it true for you.

1 I enjoy _____ (shop) *for clothes / with friends / … .*
2 I'm planning _____ (get) *a new phone / new shoes … .*
3 It's difficult _____ (choose) *clothes / music / …* for other people.
4 I know how _____ (write) a good *review / blog / … .*
5 I think it's worth _____ (spend) a lot of money on a(n) *meal in a restaurant / good haircut / … .*
6 I'm not interested in _____ (hear) about *people's problems / new stores and restaurants / … .*
7 I often *walk around the mall / look online / …* _____ (see) if there's anything I want _____ (buy).
8 _____ (go) to *language classes / the gym / …* is a good way to meet new people.

e 💬🔊 Compare your sentences in 2d. Can you find anyone who has four or more statements that are the same as yours?

3 LISTENING

a 💬🔊 You are going to hear an expert on digital marketing talking about fake reviews. What do you think he will say about these topics?

• whether you can trust reviews
• how hotels and restaurants get positive reviews
• how review sites fight against fake reviews

b ▶ 08.07 Listen to the interview. Did the expert talk about any of the things you mentioned?

c ▶08.07 Listen again and decide if the sentences are true (T) or false (F). Correct the false sentences.

1 Nearly all customers read online reviews.
2 Most people are influenced by positive reviews.
3 If a customer promises to write a positive review, they usually write it.
4 "Opinion spam" means that someone is paid to write a fake review.
5 If Amazon finds a fake reviewer, it always takes legal action.
6 TripAdvisor employs teams of people to identify fake reviewers.
7 The expert says it's best to read the negative reviews instead of the positive ones.
8 Fake reviews usually have fewer personal details than genuine ones.

d 💬🗣 Work in a small group. Discuss the questions.

1 What do you think of the expert's advice? Do you read reviews in the way he suggests?
2 When was the last time you did the following?
  • wrote a review about a place or a product
  • thought of writing a review, but forgot or decided not to

4 VOCABULARY Reporting verbs

a Complete the sentences from the interview. Which verbs from the box do you think the expert used?

---

advise   ask   were offering   persuade   promise
recommend   threaten   warn

---

1 You can _____ customers to give you a good review.
2 Customers usually _____ to write a good review, and then they forget all about it.
3 You can't really _____ a customer to write a review for you – it's up to them.
4 They found websites that _____ to write 10 positive reviews for $85.
5 They can _____ them not to continue.
6 They can _____ to take them to court.
7 I would certainly _____ reading both the good and the bad reviews.
8 And I'd also _____ people to read the review carefully to see what they really say.

b ▶08.08 Listen to the sentences and check what the expert actually said.

c Write the verbs in the chart.

Verb + infinitive	Verb + object + infinitive	Verb + verb + -ing
offer	ask	recommend

d Read these examples. Add the verbs in their base form to the chart.

1 Because there was no hot water, the hotel **agreed** to give us a 10% discount.
2 We liked the hotel so much that I **suggested** staying another night.
3 The food was so bad that I **refused** to pay for it.
4 Twice I had to **remind** the server to bring me some water.
5 My coworker **admitted** to stealing from the office.

e ≫ Now go to Vocabulary Focus 8B on p. 141.

5 SPEAKING

a You're going to talk about an experience you've had. Write notes about one of the topics below.

  • A time when you recommended something to someone (e.g., a restaurant or a movie) or someone recommended something to you
  • A time when someone warned you not to do something
  • A time when you admitted making a mistake. What had you done? How did you feel? How did other people react?
  • A time when you refused to do something. What did you refuse to do? Why did you refuse to do it?
  • A time you or someone else promised to do something but didn't do it. What was it?

b 💬🗣 Take turns talking about your experience for at least a minute. Has anyone in your group had a similar experience?

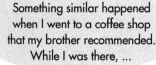
I recommended my favorite restaurant to a coworker. He went there for dinner, and later I found out that ...

Something similar happened when I went to a coffee shop that my brother recommended. While I was there, ...

8C EVERYDAY ENGLISH
On the whole, I prefer writing about current events

P /h/ and /w/
S Being vague

1 LISTENING

a 💬 Discuss the questions.

1 How do you feel before important interviews? Why?
2 What can you do to prepare for a job interview? Think of three things.

b ▶ 08.09 Listen to Part 1. Compare your ideas from 1a with those in the conversation. Then answer the questions.

1 What is Laura doing to prepare for her interview?
2 How does Laura feel about her interview? Why?
3 What job will she be interviewing for?

c ▶ 08.10 Listen to Part 2. Answer the questions.

1 How does Laura feel about the writing in her portfolio?
2 What two things does Laura ask the interviewer about?

d ▶ 08.10 Listen to Part 2 again. Complete each sentence with one or two words.

1 Laura has written about children with _____.
2 Laura's preference is to write about _____.
3 Reporters have to work locally before taking on a _____ story.
4 Reporters travel around the _____.
5 In Washington, a reporter interviewed _____.

2 USEFUL LANGUAGE Generalizing

a ▶ 08.11 Listen and complete the sentences with the phrases in the box.

generally	on the whole	as a rule	tend to	typically

1 It _____ takes a couple of years of writing at the local level …
2 Yes, _____ our writers take turns covering stories around the country …
3 But I think, _____, I prefer writing about current events …
4 _____, for example, our newest political writers _____ write about either city politics or state politics first …

b Underline the phrases for generalizing in these sentences.

1 It can be difficult to relax at the end of the day. I find my yoga class really helpful for that.
2 As a rule, I'm not very good at interviews – I get too nervous.
3 I don't usually spend much time worrying about things that haven't happened yet.

c Are the sentences in 2b true for you? If not, change them to make them true.

3 CONVERSATION SKILLS Being vague

a Replace the words in **bold** with the words in the box.

a few	things	kind

1 I prefer writing about current events – politics and that **sort** of thing.
2 You have **a couple of** features about children with learning disabilities in your portfolio.
3 I'm not very good at **stuff** like that.

b Complete the second sentence in each pair using vague language so that it means the same as the first sentence. More than one answer might be possible.

a couple of   things/stuff like that
a few   that sort/kind of thing

1 I like swimming, playing tennis, and jogging.
I like swimming and _____.
2 Everything went well except for one or two problems.
Everything went well except for _____ problems.
3 I'm going to the supermarket. I need some milk, eggs, bread, and cheese.
I'm going to the supermarket. I need some milk and _____.

4 LISTENING

a 💬 Discuss the questions.

1 How did Laura do on the job interview?
2 Do you think she will get the job? Why / Why not?

b ▶ 08.12 Listen to Part 3 and check your ideas.

c ▶ 08.13 Listen and complete the sentences.

1 Oh, it was something about my _____ of some famous journalists – what I thought of their style.
2 There's some travel, and the _____ in the office seems really nice.
3 Well, they don't _____ tell you during the interview, but … hold on, I just got an email.

5 PRONUNCIATION /h/ and /w/

a ▶ 08.14 Listen to these sentences. What sounds do the underlined words begin with?

1 Pretty well, I think, on the whole.
2 What was the question?
3 I was there for around two hours.

b ▶ 08.15 Match the words in the box with the sound each word begins with. Listen and check.

white   honest   hotel   wrap   who   work

• /h/ e.g., *happy*:
• /w/ e.g., *water*:
• first letter silent:

c ▶ 08.16 Listen to the following sentences. Choose the word you hear.

1 You can *eat / heat* the food if you like.
2 He wrote on the board *invite / in white*.
3 A few weeks ago she lost her *earring / hearing*.
4 The man you are looking for is the one in the *west / vest*.
5 I *hate / ate* the food that my daughter cooked.

6 SPEAKING

a 💬 Ask your partner for advice on one of these topics:

• a class you would like to take
• a local restaurant for a special occasion
• an area of your town/city to live in.

> I'd like to study French next year. Do you have any advice?

> I've heard that it's very difficult to be accepted into the language program. But, on the whole, the teachers are very good.

✓ UNIT PROGRESS TEST

→ **CHECK YOUR PROGRESS**

You can now do the Unit Progress Test.

1 LISTENING AND SPEAKING

a 💬 Look at the three photos of air travel below. What is happening in each photo?

b 💬 In your opinion, what are the best and worst things about air travel?

c You are going to listen to someone talking about a news story. Some of the key words from the story are in the box. What do you think happened?

> 11-year-old boy   Manchester   mother   shopping
> airport   security   plane   Rome   complained

d 💬 Compare your stories with other students.

e ▶ 08.17 Listen to the story. How close was it to your story?

f Do we know if these statements are true? Write T (true), F (false), or DK (don't know).

1 The speaker read the story in a newspaper.
2 The boy was alone in the shopping center.
3 His mother went to the airport to look for him.
4 The boy spoke to the children in the other family.
5 The boy didn't have a boarding pass.
6 They didn't count the passengers before they took off.
7 The airline offered the mother a free flight in the future.
8 It's the first time something like this has ever happened.

g ▶ 08.17 Listen again and check your answers.

h 💬 Discuss the questions.

1 Do you think something like this could happen in your country?
2 Do you think airport security in your country is
   a too strict?
   b not strict enough?
   c about right?

2 READING

a Look at the headline of a similar news story below. What do you think happened? Choose a or b.

1 a He drove the car himself.
   b He was a passenger in the car.
2 a He flew the plane himself.
   b He was a passenger on the plane.

b Read the story quickly and check your answers to 2a.

c Read the story again. Write notes about things that are the same as in the story you listened to.

13-YEAR-OLD BOY DRIVES TO AIRPORT AND FLIES ACROSS THE U.S.

Kenton Weaver is 13 years old and has no photo ID. But that didn't stop him from taking his father's car in the middle of the night, driving more than 20 miles to a Florida airport, and taking two connecting flights to San José, California. "I really enjoyed it," said Kenton.

Kenton's mother, Kim Casey, lives just half an hour from San José airport in Fresno, California, but the boy's father, Dean Weaver, thinks it was the journey itself that interested the boy. According to Dean, his son is fascinated by airplanes. "He'll do anything to go to an airport," Dean said. "He wants to be a pilot."

Kenton did not own a credit card, passport, driver's license, or photo ID of any kind. Yet he was able somehow to buy a plane ticket, go through airport security, fly to Chicago, and catch his connecting flight to San José without any problems. His father said it is possible Kenton used the numbers from one of his own credit cards to buy the ticket online.

3 WRITING SKILLS Summarizing information

a Read a summary of the news story. Which words in **bold** tell us … ?

1 that the person is reporting a story they read or heard about somewhere
2 that the person is commenting on what happened

There was an **incredible** story in the newspaper last week. **Apparently**, a 13-year-old boy took his father's car, drove it to the airport, and then took two flights from Florida to California to see his mother, who lives there. **Amazingly**, he did all this without a credit card, ID, or driver's license. **It seems that** he used his father's credit card number to buy the plane ticket online, and no one asked him any questions. **Fortunately**, they found him and everything was all right in the end.

b ▶08.17 Listen to the story again. Write down any more words used to comment on the story.

c Compare the sentences below with the highlighted sentence in the summary in 3a. Answer questions 1–4.

A boy of 13 took his father's car. The boy drove it to the airport. The boy took two flights from Florida to California. The boy flew there to see his mother. His mother lives in California.

1 How many sentences are in 3c?
2 What words are added to connect these sentences in 3a?
3 What words are left out or changed in the summary in 3a? Why?
4 Why is the summary in 3a better than the sentences in 3c?

d Here is a different summary of the same news story. Connect the sentences to make four or five sentences. Use the words in the box to help you (you can use the words more than once).

and   before   but   who   with

I read an incredible news story about a boy.
Apparently he flew alone from Florida to California.
He was only 13.
He managed to fly alone across America.
He even changed planes in Chicago.
He bought a ticket online.
He used his father's credit card number.
No one at the airport asked him any questions.
He even took his father's car.
He parked it in the airport parking lot.
He got on the plane.

e 💬 Work in pairs and compare your summaries. Are they the same?

4 WRITING An email about a news story

a 💬 Work in pairs. Choose one of the headlines below or a story in the news at the moment. Discuss and write notes about what happened.

POLICE FIND MISSING GIRL

Tiger Escapes from Zoo

MAN JUMPS FROM PLANE – and SURVIVES

SURFER ESCAPES SHARK ATTACK

b Work in pairs. Write an email to a friend, summarizing the story in a few sentences. Include words or phrases to comment on the story.

c 💬 Work with another pair. Read each other's emails and answer the questions.

1 Is the information clear and in a logical order?
2 Is the amount of information right?
3 Are there too many or too few sentences? Are they connected in the best way?
4 Can you improve the summary?

d 💬 Tell another pair about your news story.

UNIT 8
Review and extension

1 GRAMMAR

a Read the text and <u>underline</u> the correct answers.

"Internet users worry about ¹*to lose / losing* private information online, but they don't mind ²*to see / seeing* advertisements that are personally directed at them." That's what the Digital Advertising Alliance discovered when they conducted a survey ³*to find out / finding out* how consumers feel about targeted advertising. Only 4% said they didn't like the idea of ⁴*to get / getting* targeted advertising.

Consumers seem ⁵*to understand / understanding* that ads make it possible ⁶*to have / having* free websites: 75% of people said that they didn't want ⁷*to pay / paying* for websites with no advertising on them.

b Complete the reported speech.

1 "I'll never go to that hairdresser again," you said.
   You said _____ to that hairdresser again.
2 Kate asked John, "What are you going to buy?"
   Kate asked John _____ to buy.
3 The editor said to me, "You may need to rewrite this story."
   The editor told me _____ this story.
4 The interviewer asked me, "Have you ever written a blog?"
   The interviewer asked me _____ a blog.

2 VOCABULARY

a Complete the sentences with a suitable noun. Sometimes more than one answer is possible.

1 You know so much about politics. You should create your own _____ about it.
2 I'm really excited about this project. We brainstormed some amazing _____ in the meeting today.
3 If you're worried, you should have a _____ about it with your manager.
4 I watched a really funny _____ of that new comedy series last night. Did you see it?
5 I spend too much time checking my _____ on social media, but I love to stay up to date with what's happening.

b Write a sentence with each of the reporting verbs below.

1 advise
2 warn
3 threaten
4 recommend
5 promise

3 WORDPOWER *in/on* + noun

a Look at the phrases in the box and <u>underline</u> the correct words in the rules.

| on the label   on a website   in capital letters |
| in cash   in the photo   in a magazine |

1 We use *in / on* + flat surfaces like *wall*, *page*, and *screen*.
2 We use *in / on* + *movie* and *picture* (when we talk about what they show).
3 We use *in / on* + *the Internet, the radio, TV, Facebook,* and *Twitter*.
4 We use *in / on* + written and printed material (e.g., *the newspaper, a sentence, an email*).
5 We use *in / on* with sizes (e.g., *12, medium*), currencies (e.g., *dollars, yen*), and before *stock*.

b Complete the sentences with *in* or *on*.

1 What can you see _____ the picture?
2 I have some photos of Paul _____ my phone.
3 The answer was _____ the first paragraph.
4 Was it strange to see your name _____ print?
5 The full article is _____ page 4.
6 They were talking about his new movie _____ the radio.
7 Did you pay _____ cash?
8 How much is $30 _____ euros?
9 The words "Not for sale" were _____ the sign.
10 **A** I'm looking for these shoes _____ size 9.
    B I'm afraid we don't have them _____ stock at the moment.
11 Your seat number is _____ the ticket.
12 If you write _____ pencil, it doesn't matter if you make a mistake.

c 💬 Take turns testing each other on the phrases.

The Internet.

On the Internet.

⟲ CAN DO OBJECTIVES

■ Talk about movies and TV

■ Give extra information

■ Recommend and respond
to recommendations

■ Write an article

UNIT

9

ENTERTAINMENT

GETTING STARTED

a 💬 Look at the photo and answer the questions.

1 Who are these people?
2 What are they doing and why?
3 What do you think the people watching think of the performance? Why?

b 💬 Are there similar street entertainers in your area? Do you like them?

c 💬 What other kinds of street entertainers can you think of? Which ones do you like or not like?

9A BINGE WATCHING HAS BEEN CRITICIZED BY DOCTORS

1 LISTENING

a 💬 Trailers are ads for movies or TV shows that are coming soon. Discuss the questions about trailers.

1 Do you watch trailers for movies and TV shows? Why / Why not?
2 Do trailers usually make you want to watch the movie or series? Why / Why not?
3 Think of a time you watched a movie / TV series because you liked the trailer. Were you pleased or disappointed? Explain your answer.
4 Which of these things make a good trailer? Are any other things important?
   ☐ a lot of short scenes
   ☐ one or two longer scenes
   ☐ only scenes with music – no talking
   ☐ a description of what the movie is about

b ▶09.01 Listen to Ava and Lucas talking about trailers. Answer the questions.

1 Who was disappointed? _____
2 Who talks about some research? _____
3 What organizations use the research? _____

c ▶09.01 Listen again and answer the questions.

1 What does Ava think is a key problem with trailers?
2 Why is she surprised that they are expensive to make?
3 How did researchers check the facial expressions of people watching trailers?
4 What did this tell the researchers?
5 How did they use this information?
6 What are two important features of a successful trailer?
7 Who isn't worried about the way movie companies make trailers? Why not?

d 💬 Think of a trailer you have seen recently. Did it follow the structure Lucas describes? Did it make you want to watch the movie or TV show? Why / Why not?

2 VOCABULARY -ed / -ing adjectives

a <u>Underline</u> the correct adjectives to complete the sentences.

1 I watched this true crime show last night – it was really *disappointing* / *disappointed*.

2 They make TV shows and movies look a lot more *interesting* / *interested* than they are.
3 So, from the facial expressions, they could figure out whether the people were *amusing* / *amused* or *fascinating* / *fascinated* or *boring* / *bored*.
4 But it also meant movie companies could use the information to come up with a model for making really *motivating* / *motivated* trailers.
5 It's kind of *depressing* / *depressed* – more algorithms to make us do things.
6 And I'm always *interesting* / *interested* in finding out about the latest marketing trick.

b Look at the two examples. Which adjective in **bold** … ?

I found the movie **boring**.
I was so **bored** by the movie that I fell asleep.
1 describes how the speaker felt _____
2 describes what the movie was like _____

c ▶09.02 **Pronunciation** Listen to the -ed adjectives. How is the final -ed pronounced in each one? Complete the chart with the words in the box.

disappointed   interested   amused
fascinated   bored   motivated   depressed

/d/	/t/	/ɪd/

d Complete the sentences with the -ed or -ing form of the adjectives in the box.

disappoint   fascinate   interest   amuse   motivate   depress

1 Nicole and I are going to a concert next week. Are you _____ in coming, too?
2 Some people find winter sad and _____, but I like it.
3 That new restaurant was a little _____ – the food wasn't nearly as good as the review said.
4 I thought Chiara would laugh at my joke, but she wasn't _____.
5 My test scores were high, so I feel very _____ to keep studying hard.
6 The book tells an absolutely _____ story of growing up in New York. It was an amazing read!

e Write notes about these topics.

- a time you felt disappointed
- a book or movie that you found interesting
- a movie or TV show that you find amusing
- something you find motivating to work/study hard for
- something you think is boring
- what you do when you feel depressed

f 💬 Take turns telling each other about each topic. Ask your partner questions about their ideas.

3 READING

a 💬 Discuss the questions.

1 Do you sometimes watch three or more episodes of a TV show one after the other? Why / Why not?

2 What are some of the advantages and disadvantages of watching TV in this way?

b Read the article. What advantages and disadvantages does it mention? Were they the same as your ideas in question 2?

c 💬 Read the article again and write notes for each category below. Compare your ideas with your partner.

1 I didn't know about this.
2 I agree with this.
3 I don't agree with this.
4 This is something I've done or felt.

To **BINGE** or Not to **BINGE** ...

Last week, a new TV series was uploaded to your streaming service, and it's great. Two nights ago, you watched the first episode, and then last night you watched episode two. It ended with a really exciting cliffhanger* and you didn't know what was going to happen next – you just had to watch the next episode. And then the next. Then suddenly it was 1:30 a.m., and today you're sitting at work feeling exhausted. Sound familiar? Admit it – you've been binge watching.

In the past, TV viewing was controlled by what was on the TV channels. But things have changed with the growth of streaming services like Netflix and Amazon Prime. Instead of waiting a week for each new episode of a TV show to become available, we can now get them all at once, and watch as many episodes as we like. In particular, young people are attracted to TV series they can binge on. In a recent study in the U.S., 76% of adults between the ages of 18 and 29 admitted canceling other plans in order to stay up all night and binge watch a show.

So why do we do it? The simple answer is that it makes us feel good. When we binge watch, we get a sense of enjoyment due to the fact that dopamine, a natural feel-good hormone, is released into our brains. Binge watchers say that a good TV series is a great way to relax and escape from some of the stress of our day-to-day lives. They also like the fact that episodes are long and are a pleasant change from the kind of bite-sized entertainment that is found on social media.

However, binge watching has been criticized by doctors and other health experts. They say it encourages lack of activity, which can lead to poor fitness and problems with weight. They also say it can have a negative effect on our sleep. So, having stayed up until 1:30 a.m. watching your favorite show, you then have trouble getting to sleep. Finally, binge watching can cause psychological problems. Some viewers talk about a sense of loneliness and emptiness when a series ends, and they say that binge watching is an addictive behavior.

*****cliffhanger** a movie, TV show, or story that is exciting because the ending is uncertain until it happens

The experts say that many of the harmful effects of binge viewing can be reduced by following some simple rules:

▶ Set a daily time limit on the number of hours you watch TV and stick to it.

▶ Choose a room where you watch TV, and only watch it there, but don't choose your bedroom – that's for sleeping.

▶ Watch an episode from three different shows and not the same one – if you think you need to watch three episodes in an evening.

▶ Take a break between episodes and do something different for 10 minutes.

▶ Stop watching anything 30 minutes before you go to bed.

Many TV streamers don't believe that binge watching is harmful. They say it's like reading a book you can't put down, and that's never been considered a health problem. You get lost in the story and you have to keep going. These TV series are also like books, because to really appreciate them, you need to stay with the story and feel they are part of your life.

Whether you see binge watching as harmful or harmless, the opportunity to stream your favorite show on demand isn't going away any time soon. More and more series are being made by a wider range of streaming companies. The writing and the production quality are improving all the time. These shows are made to pull us in and keep us in front of our TVs.

4 GRAMMAR The passive

a Look at the examples of the passive in bold and underline the correct words to complete the rules.

Last week, a new TV series **was uploaded** *to your streaming service.*
Young people **are attracted** *to TV series they can binge on.*

We often use the passive when:
1 we *know / don't know* who did an action
2 it's *obvious / not obvious* who did an action
3 it's *important / not important* who did an action

The first episode **was directed by** *Martin Scorsese.*
The whole episode **was filmed with** *a cell-phone camera.*

4 We can use *by / with* + noun after a passive verb to tell what was used to do the action.
5 We can use *by / with* + noun after a passive verb to tell who/what did the action.

b Read the sentences. Underline the passive verbs and circle the active verbs.
1 In the past, TV viewing was controlled by TV channels.
2 Some viewers talk about a sense of loneliness and emptiness when a series ends.
3 Dopamine, a natural feel-good hormone, is released into our brains.
4 Seventy-six percent of adults between the ages of 18 and 29 admitted canceling other plans in order to stay up all night and binge watch a show.
5 However, binge watching has been criticized by doctors and other health experts.
6 Finally, binge watching can cause psychological problems.
7 The experts say that many of the harmful effects of binge viewing can be reduced by following some simple rules.
8 More and more series are being made by a wider range of streaming companies.
9 The writing and the production quality are improving all the time.

c Which of the passive forms are ... ?
1 ☐ simple present   4 ☐ present perfect
2 ☐ present continuous 5 ☐ a modal verb
3 ☐ simple past

d Now go to Grammar Focus 9A on p. 160.

e ≫ Communication 9A 💬 You are going to read about video and audio streaming services. Student A: Read the text below and choose the correct form of the verbs to complete the sentences. Student B: Go to p. 131. Read the text and choose the correct form of the verbs to complete the sentences.

Student A

Video streaming facts and figures
Video *has streamed / has been streamed* in the U.S. since the early 1990s. It *started / was started* by a company called Starlight Networks. Now the largest streaming site in the world is YouTube, which *has / is had* over a billion users worldwide. The global video streaming service *values / is valued* at about $120 billion. An average U.S. viewer *spends / is spent* 15 hours a week watching streamed video.

f 💬 Work in pairs. Share the information you learned about streaming services.

5 SPEAKING

a You are going to recommend a movie or TV show that you like. Write notes on as many of the questions as you can.
- What is it called?
- What kind of movie or show is it?
- What happens? Who are the main characters?
- When and where is it set?
- Who directed it?
- Is it based on a book or a true story?
- Who is in it – any famous actors or celebrities?
- Does it have special effects?

b Write three reasons why you like this movie or TV show.

c 💬 Take turns recommending your movie or TV show. Have you watched the movies or TV shows you hear about? If so, do you like them, too? If not, would you like to watch them? Why / Why not?

9B I WENT TO A CONCERT THAT CHANGED MY LIFE

Learn to give extra information

- **G** Defining and non-defining relative clauses
- **V** Music; Word-building (nouns)

1 VOCABULARY Music

a 💬 What's happening in the photos below? Match the words to photos 1–3.

audience guitar DJ play live
festival musician orchestra perform

b ▶ 09.04 Listen to four clips of music and <u>underline</u> the correct words.

1 They are playing *live / in a recording studio*.
2 You can hear a *DJ / musician*.
3 Someone is *performing / enjoying* a piece of music.
4 You can hear *a choir / an orchestra*.

c 💬 Discuss the questions. Use a dictionary to check the words in **bold**.

1 When and where did you last listen to a song?
2 What are your favorite **albums** and your favorite **tracks**?
3 Do you like making **playlists**?
4 When and where did you last sing or play a musical **instrument**?

2 LISTENING

a 💬 How many different musical experiences can you think of? Write a list.

going to concerts, singing in a choir …

b 💬 Compare your lists. Which of these experiences do you like taking part in or going to? Why?

c ▶ 09.05 Listen to three people talk about musical experiences that changed their lives. Match the speakers with photos a–c.

Annie _____ Jeff _____ Erica _____

d ▶ 09.05 Listen again and write notes in the chart.

	What kind of music do they talk about?	What or where was the event?	How did it change their life?
Annie			
Jeff			
Erica			

e 💬 Talk about which of the musical experiences you would like to have. Explain your answer.

3 GRAMMAR Defining and non-defining relative clauses

a   Look at the <u>underlined</u> defining relative clauses. Circle the noun phrase that each relative clause tells you about.

A. *Defining relative clauses*

1   Samba is (a kind of Brazilian music) that/which also has African rhythms.
2   It's a drum <u>you play with your hands</u>.
3   I was sitting next to one of the people <u>who was in my group</u>.
4   They were all about the place <u>where he grew up</u>.

B. *Non-defining relative clauses*

5   I was with my brother and a friend of his, <u>who was older than me</u>, and we were listening to Jay-Z.
6   I started noticing the words, <u>which were really different from the songs I normally listened to</u>.

b   Answer the questions.

1   Which kind of relative clause, defining (*D*) or non-defining (*ND*), ... ?
   ☐ defines what the noun phrase means and makes it more specific
   ☐ only adds extra information about the noun phrase
   ☐ has a comma before it, and sometimes after it
   ☐ has no comma before it

2   Where does a relative clause come in a sentence?
   a   immediately after the noun phrase it refers to
   b   always at the end of the sentence

3   Make a list of the relative pronouns in 3a.
   that/which, _____, _____

4   Look at the sentence and complete the rule.
   It's a drum (that/which) you play with your hands.
   In *defining / non-defining* relative clauses, you can leave out the pronoun if it is the *subject / object* of the relative clause.

c   ▶ 09.06 Pronunciation Listen to the sentences. In which sentence do you hear a pause before the relative pronoun in **bold**?
1   People **who** sing a lot always seem happy.
2   Carly, **who**'s a fantastic singer, works in a café during the day.

d   ≫ Now go to Grammar Focus 9B on p. 160.

e   💬 Take turns describing the words in the box using a sentence with a defining relative clause. Guess which word your partner is describing.

| album | audience | choir | concert | DJ | festival |
| musician | orchestra | playlist | track | guitarist | |

It's something that you can download.

No, it's something that you can find on an album.

An album?

A track!

f   Add a non-defining relative clause to each of these sentences. Use *who*, *which* or *where*.
1   The concert at the Town Hall, ... , was a little disappointing.
2   He learned to play the guitar from his uncle, ...
3   There's a good café near here called *The Music Room*, ...
4   They decided to sell their piano, ...

g   💬 Work in small groups. Read out loud only the relative clause you added. Can the others guess which sentence it goes with?

The THREE BEST MUSIC FESTIVALS
You've Probably Never Heard Of

FUJI ROCK FESTIVAL, Japan
A celebration of rock and electronic music at the foot of Mount Fuji

This is Japan's largest outdoor music event. It's held every year at the Naeba Ski Resort. You can enjoy the beauty of the forests and rivers as you walk (often a very long way!) from one stage to another. This is one of the world's safest and most environmentally friendly festivals, which is probably why everyone's happiness and creativity levels are so high!

Past performers include: Kendrick Lamar, Gorillaz, N.E.R.D.

ROSKILDE, Denmark
A rock festival that gives all its profits to charity

Here, you can enjoy performances of rock, punk, heavy metal, hip-hop, indie, and music from around the world. The organizers donate all the money they make to projects that develop society and culture.

Don't forget that summer days are long in Denmark. It doesn't get dark until 11 p.m., and it starts getting light at 3:30 a.m.

Past performers include: Metallica, Bruce Springsteen, Rihanna

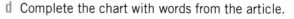

4 READING AND VOCABULARY
Word-building (nouns)

a 💬 Discuss the questions.

1 Have you ever been to a music festival?
2 If so, what kind of music was there? Did you enjoy it? Why / Why not?
3 If not, do you know of any music festivals you would like to go to? What are they like?

b Read "The Three Best Music Festivals You've Probably Never Heard Of." Which festival would you rather go to? Why?

c Read the article again and match the comments with the festivals. Write *F* (Fuji Rock Festival), *R* (Roskilde), or *C* (Comunité Festival).

1 ☐ "Even the toilet paper is made from recycled cups from last year's festival!"
2 ☐ "I'm glad I took a good pair of walking boots with me."
3 ☐ "The nights were so short!"
4 ☐ "I was happy to get away from huge crowds of people."
5 ☐ "It's really nice to know that all the money goes to good causes."
6 ☐ "The water was so clear!"

COMUNITÉ FESTIVAL, Mexico
Eco-friendly festival in the Mexican jungle

This is a small-scale festival where you can enjoy Latin American, electronic, and dance music in the jungle atmosphere of the Gulf of Mexico. If it gets too hot, just dive into one of the natural freshwater pools around the site, or head off to a nearby beach. The festival is held every January, and some of the money goes toward protecting coral reefs in the Caribbean.

Past performers include: James Holden, Auntie Flo, Kaitlin Aurelia Smith

d Complete the chart with words from the article.

Adjective	Noun		Verb
beautiful	1		
	2		celebrate
charitable	3		
creative	4		create
cultural	5		
	6		develop
happy	7		
musical	8	(person)	
organized	9	(person)	organize
	10	(person)	perform
	11		

e ▶09.08 **Pronunciation** Listen to the words in 4d. Notice how the stress sometimes changes position as we change the form of the word. Mark the stress on each word.

f ▶09.08 Listen again and practice saying the words.

g Write the noun forms of the words. Use one suffix from the box for each pair of words, and make spelling changes if necessary.

-ance/-ence -(a)tion -er/-or -ity -ist -ness -ty

1 loyal, honest: loyalty, _____
2 fit, sad: _____ , _____
3 able, responsible: _____ , _____
4 design, act: _____ , _____
5 appear, patient: _____ , _____
6 piano, guitar: _____ , _____
7 locate, relax: _____ , _____

h 💬 Talk about which of the qualities in the box are important for the people 1–4. Which qualities are not needed? Say why.

beauty creativity honesty intelligence
kindness musical ability responsibility

1 a pop singer   2 a friend   3 a teacher   4 a politician

5 SPEAKING

a You are going to talk about an interesting or exciting experience in your life that involved music. Write notes on the questions below.

1 What happened?
2 When was it?
3 Who was with you?
4 Why was it important?
5 Why have you remembered it?

b 💬 Take turns talking about your experiences and asking follow-up questions.

> I went to hear a band I've been a fan of for years ...

9C EVERYDAY ENGLISH
It's supposed to be really good

1 LISTENING

a 💬 Discuss the questions.

1 How often do you have an evening out with friends? What do you usually do?

2 How easy is it to organize an evening out with your friends? Do you all have the same interests? Do you ever disagree about what you want to do?

3 Look at the photos and the activities in the box. Which activities do you enjoy?

> a meal in a restaurant   a horror movie
> a meal at a friend's house   a pop concert
> hanging out at the mall   playing online games with friends

b ▶09.09 Listen to Part 1. Two friends, Renata and Amanda, are talking about weekend plans. Which activities are mentioned? What do they decide to do in the end?

c ▶09.09 Listen to Part 1 again. Who …

1 suggests going to a jazz club? *Renata / Amanda*

2 suggests going to a classical music festival? *Renata / Amanda*

3 doesn't like classical music? *Amanda / Caleb*

4 suggests hearing a local rock band? *Milo / Renata*

5 hasn't gone to a rock concert in 10 years? *Caleb / Milo*

2 USEFUL LANGUAGE
Recommending and responding

a ▶09.09 Listen to Part 1 again and check (✓) the phrases you hear.

1 ☐ That's a great idea.

2 ☐ I heard it was excellent.

3 ☐ It was highly recommended by …

4 ☐ It's supposed to be really nice.

5 ☐ I'm not a big fan of classical music.

6 ☐ Why don't we go to the classical music festival at the university?

7 ☐ They have great reviews.

8 ☐ I think you'd love it.

9 ☐ I doubt he would be interested, though.

10 ☐ It sounds really interesting.

b Which phrases in 2a … ?

1 give a recommendation or opinion

2 respond to a recommendation

c 💬 Work in groups of three. Use the diagram below to have a conversation.

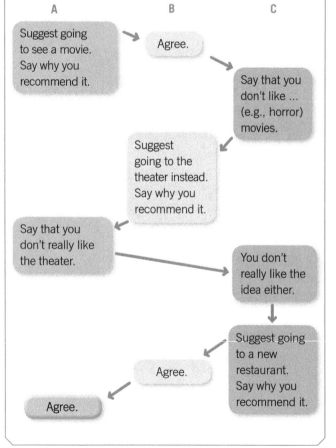

A — Suggest going to see a movie. Say why you recommend it.

B — Agree.

C — Say that you don't like … (e.g., horror) movies.

B — Suggest going to the theater instead. Say why you recommend it.

A — Say that you don't really like the theater.

C — You don't really like the idea either.

C — Suggest going to a new restaurant. Say why you recommend it.

B — Agree.

A — Agree.

3 PRONUNCIATION Showing contrast

a ▶09.10 Listen to the following sentence. Which word is stressed?

I'm not a big fan of classical music.

b ▶09.11 Listen to these conversations. Decide which words are stressed more in each sentence.

1 **A** Why don't we go to the classical music festival at the university? It's supposed to be really good.

   B I'm not a big fan of classical music. I'm sure Milo would like it, but not me.
   (= It's Milo who likes classical music, not me.)

2 **A** You'd think it would be easier to find something we all like to do.

   B I know, right? Milo says they play rock, but it's kind of retro 1980s, so Caleb should like it, right?
   (= It's retro music that Caleb likes, not rock.)

When we want to show a contrast (emphasize that something is different), we stress that word more.

c 💬 Work in pairs. Take turns asking the questions and replying, showing contrast by stressing a word.

1 Did you buy the red shoes? (blue)
2 Did you go to the movies with John? (museum)
3 Did you see John? (Chris)

4 CONVERSATION SKILLS
Asking someone to wait

a ▶09.12 Listen to the things Amanda and Renata said. Complete the sentences.

1 **AMANDA** _____ on. Milo's texting me now.
2 **RENATA** Just a _____ . Let me check with him.

b Complete the chart with the words in the box.

| check   hang   please   second   wait |

¹ _____ on Just ² _____	a minute / a ³ _____ / a moment.
One moment, ⁴ _____ .	
Let me ⁵ _____ (for you).	

c Which expression is more formal?

d 💬 Work in pairs. Follow the instructions and have a conversation.

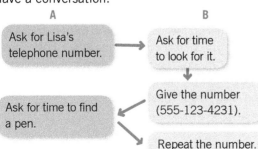

A	B
Ask for Lisa's telephone number.	Ask for time to look for it.
Ask for time to find a pen.	Give the number (555-123-4231). Repeat the number.

5 LISTENING

a 💬 Amanda said Caleb should wear something cool. Look at the clothes below.

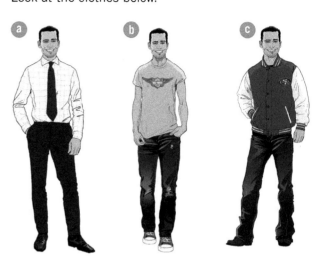

Which outfit do you think is the coolest? Which do you think Caleb will wear?

b ▶09.13 Listen to Part 2 and check your ideas. What does Renata think of Caleb's clothes?

c 💬 Discuss the questions.

1 Do you usually spend a lot of time choosing what to wear when you go out? Why / Why not?
2 What kind of clothes do people in your area wear when they go out for the evening (e.g., to a restaurant, to a concert, to the mall, to hang out with friends)?

6 SPEAKING

≫ Communication 9C 💬 You're going to have a conversation about what to do today. Student A: Read the information below. Student B: Go to p. 131.

Student A
• You would like to go to an exhibition of modern art.
• You just ate, so you don't want to go out for a meal.
• Someone gave you an ad for a photography exhibition. You have the ad in your bag.

We could go to the modern art exhibition. It's supposed to be really interesting.

That sounds OK, but I'm not a big fan of modern art.

✓ UNIT PROGRESS TEST

→ CHECK YOUR PROGRESS

You can now do the Unit Progress Test.

9D SKILLS FOR WRITING
I like going out, but …

Learn to write an article
W Contrasting ideas;
The structure of an article

1 SPEAKING AND LISTENING

a 💬 Look at photos a–e. If you could win free tickets to go to one of the events, which would you choose? Why?

b ▶ 09.14 Listen to Anna and her friend Camila. Answer the questions.

1 Who has tickets to the Kendrick Lamar concert?
2 Who doesn't want to go?
3 Why doesn't she want to go?

c Write notes about the topics below. What are the positive and negative points of these ways of listening to music?

- live performances (concerts, etc.)
- recorded performances (albums, movies, etc.)

d 💬 Discuss your opinions. Do you prefer live or recorded music? Why?

2 READING

a Read Julia's blog, "Why I Prefer to Stay at Home." What is her main point?

1 Movies are too expensive, and it's cheaper to stay at home.
2 It's more comfortable and convenient to watch movies and TV series at home.
3 Movies are less satisfying than TV shows.

b Read the blog again and answer the questions.

1 What annoys Julia about movie audiences?
2 Why were the couple sitting behind her rude?
3 What does she do if she finds a movie boring?
4 Why is the length of a TV series sometimes a good thing?

≡ ⌂   💬 ↻ ☰ ✉

Why I Prefer to Stay at Home

1 What was your last experience at the movies like? I remember the expensive tickets, the long lines, and the uncomfortable seats. Does this sound familiar? I love going out to see my friends and going to parties. I like having fun. However, I don't really enjoy going to the movie theater anymore.

2 To me, the main problem with going to the movies is the audience. Although many people say that seeing a movie in the theater is a good chance to go out and be sociable, I really hate listening to other people's comments. The last time I went to the movies, there was a couple who commented loudly on everything. They laughed at everything in the movie, really loudly – even at things that weren't funny! I politely asked them to be quiet. Despite this, they continued as if they were watching their own TV. If I watch something at home, I can invite my friends and spend time with people I know and like rather than sitting near noisy strangers.

3 Another reason for staying at home is convenience. I like to watch movies and TV shows when I want to watch them, not at specific times. In spite of my love of movies and TV shows, I don't enjoy all of them. If I'm at home, I can stop the movie and watch something else, or I can skip through the boring parts. For example, I was really disappointed with a movie I saw last night – so I just turned it off!

4 While I watch a lot of movies, I also watch a lot of TV shows online now. I really enjoy watching a whole series. It gives characters time to develop in interesting and unexpected ways. In fact, there are so many great TV shows to watch, I hardly have time to go out to the movies.

5 So these days, when my friends invite me to go to the movies, I usually say, "No, thanks." I really do prefer to watch movies and TV shows at home. I can choose what I want to watch, I can choose the time when I want to watch it, and I can choose who I watch it with. The question really is: why should I go out?

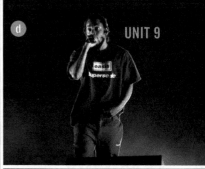

3 WRITING SKILLS Contrasting ideas; The structure of an article

a In the example below, *however* introduces a contrast. Find more examples of expressions used to contrast ideas in Julia's blog.

I like having fun. **However**, I don't really enjoy going to the movie theater anymore.

b Complete the rules and examples with the words in the box. Use each word twice.

although   despite   however   in spite of   while

- *I enjoy movies.* ¹_____, *I think I prefer TV series.*
We can use ²_____ at the beginning of a sentence. It contrasts with an idea in the previous sentence.

- ³_____ / ⁴_____ *movie theaters have become more comfortable, they're not as comfortable as my sofa.*
We can use ⁵_____ and ⁶_____ to introduce a contrasting idea. They are followed by a clause with a verb.

- *The price of a movie ticket has gone up recently.*
⁷_____ / ⁸_____ *the cost, I still love going to the movies.*
We can use ⁹_____ and ¹⁰_____ to introduce a contrasting idea. They are followed by a noun or pronoun.

c Match ideas 1–6 with a contrasting idea a–f. Connect the ideas using the words in parentheses in the correct position. Write only one sentence, if possible.

1 ☐ I was given two free tickets to a jazz concert (However)
2 ☐ music is something we normally listen to at home (Although)
3 ☐ TV screens have gotten bigger and bigger (Although)
4 ☐ the beat is very important in hip-hop music (While)
5 ☐ the convenience of watching a movie at home (In spite of)
6 ☐ my love of special effects (Despite)

a the words are just as important.
b I don't like that kind of music, so I'll give them away.
c there's nothing like the big screen at a movie theater.
d I still want movies to have a good story and good acting.
e it's always interesting to watch musicians perform.
f I prefer to see movies at a theater.

d Look at paragraphs 2–4 in Julia's blog. What is the main idea of each paragraph? Choose a or b.

Paragraph 2:
a movie theater audiences   b being polite in movie theaters
Paragraph 3:
a boring movies   b the convenience of staying at home
Paragraph 4:
a the length of TV series   b an alternative to watching movies

e 💬 Discuss the questions about Julia's blog.

1 Is the main idea mentioned at the beginning or in the middle of the paragraph?
2 Does Julia sometimes use examples?
3 How does Julia get the reader's attention in paragraph 1, the introduction?
4 In paragraph 5, the conclusion, does Julia introduce new ideas? Why / Why not?

4 WRITING An article

a You are going to write an article about a kind of entertainment you love or hate. Choose one of the topics below or your own idea. Then write notes about questions 1–4.

- music concerts in stadiums or in small clubs
- watching sports in a stadium or live on TV
- classical music or pop music

1 What's your opinion about this topic?
2 What experience do you have with it?
3 What other things do you know about it?
4 What do other people often say about it?

b 💬 Compare your ideas with a partner.

c Plan your article. Follow these instructions:

1 Write down the main ideas of the article.
2 Write down different points for each idea.
3 Think of any examples from your experience.

d Write your article. Make sure you write an introduction and conclusion. Remember to use words or phrases to show contrast.

1 GRAMMAR

a Read the text and underline the correct words.

Can you imagine a movie ¹*who / that* had no music? It would be very boring. Here are two talented movie composers ²*what / that* everyone should know about.

John Williams ³*sees / is seen* as one of the greatest movie composers of all time. He ⁴*has nominated / has been nominated* for more awards than anyone else, apart from Walt Disney. Williams, ⁵*whose / who* music can be heard in the *Harry Potter* and *Star Wars* movies, is most famous for working with director Steven Spielberg.

The music for *Titanic*, *The Amazing Spider-Man*, and more than 100 other movies was written ⁶*with / by* pianist and composer James Horner. In his compositions, Horner often uses Celtic music, ⁷*which / that* is traditional music from Western Europe.

b Complete the second sentence so that it means the same as the first sentence (or pair of sentences). Use three words in each space.

1 The movie was based on a book. I loved it when I was a child.
   The movie was based on a _____ when I was a child.

2 That's the place. The final scene was filmed there.
   That's the place _____ scene was filmed.

3 *The Crimes of Grindelwald* is the second movie in the *Fantastic Beasts* series. *The Crimes of Grindelwald* came out in 2018.
   The Crimes of Grindelwald, _____ in 2018, is the second movie in the *Fantastic Beasts* series.

4 People are forgetting many traditional folk songs.
   Many traditional folk songs _____ .

5 They were recording the concert when I was there.
   The concert _____ when I was there.

2 VOCABULARY

a Read the text and complete the adjectives with the correct ending, *-ed* or *-ing*.

I stayed at home and binge watched a new animal documentary series this weekend. It was ¹fascinat____ . I've always been ²interest____ in nature, and I wasn't ³disappoint____ . The final episode was a little ⁴bor____ , though. It was all about plastic pollution. I mean, I know it is important to get that message out there, but it was pretty ⁵depress____ to watch. I suppose I am more ⁶motivat____ to recycle; it's just that I prefer episodes that are ⁷excit____ and dramatic.

b Complete the sentences with noun forms of the words in parentheses.

1 The festival is a ____ of music from different cultures. (celebrate)

2 We'd like to thank the ____ for all their hard work in preparing the show. (organize)

3 This movie shows the ____ of the Pacific Islands. (beautiful)

4 The ____ are preparing for their ____ this evening. (music; perform)

3 WORDPOWER *see, look at, watch, hear, listen to*

a Match questions 1–8 with responses a–h.

1 ☐ Amy! Amy! Why isn't she answering?
2 ☐ What's that noise?
3 ☐ Have you found another painting?
4 ☐ Are they dancing?
5 ☐ What's that light in the sky?
6 ☐ Do you **see** what I mean?
7 ☐ Are you going to **see** the doctor?
8 ☐ Have you **seen** the latest *Marvel* movie?

a Yes, I have an appointment tomorrow.
b I don't **see** anything.
c No, I don't understand.
d Yes, I **watched** it with Brendan.
e I don't **hear** anything.
f She's **listening to** music.
g Yes, come and **look at** it! It's amazing!
h Yes, come and **watch**.

b Add the words in **bold** in 3a to the chart.

1	pay attention to something because of its appearance (e.g., a photo, a flower)
2	pay attention to something because of the movement (e.g., a movie)
3	be able to recognize sights
	watch something that's moving, or attend some entertainment event
	understand
	visit
4	be able to recognize sounds
5	pay attention to sounds

c 💬 Underline the correct words. Then discuss the questions.

1 How often do you *watch / look at* old photos of yourself?
2 When did you last *see / watch* the dentist?
3 What music do you *listen to / hear* when you're in a bad mood?
4 *Watch / Look* out the window. What do you *see / look at*?
5 *Listen / Hear*. What do you *listen / hear*?
6 If you *listened to / heard* a strange noise in the night, would you go and *watch / see* what it was?
7 What is the worst movie you've ever *seen / looked at*?

⟳ REVIEW YOUR PROGRESS

How well did you do in this unit? Write 3, 2, or 1 for each objective.
3 = very well   2 = well   1 = not so well

I CAN ...	
talk about movies and TV	☐
give extra information	☐
recommend and respond to recommendations	☐
write an article.	☐

✪ CAN DO OBJECTIVES

- Talk about new things it would be good to do
- Talk about imagined past events
- Talk about possible problems and reassure someone
- Write an email with advice

UNIT 10

OPPORTUNITIES

GETTING STARTED

a 💬 What kind of event can you see in the photo? How are these events similar or different in your country?

b 💬 Ask and answer the questions.

1 What opportunities can going to college give you?
2 What opportunities have you had in your life? For example, think about education, travel, meeting people, and work.

3 Describe a time when you did something that you found scary or difficult (e.g., skydiving, giving a speech, or performing in a show). How did this experience make you feel? Explain your answer.

10A | IF I WERE IN BETTER SHAPE, I'D DO IT!

1 SPEAKING

a 💬 Look at photos a–c.
1 What is happening (or going to happen) in each photo?
2 How are the people in each photo feeling?

b Add more sports in these categories.
- winter sports: *skiing, ...*
- ball sports: *tennis, ...*
- water sports: *surfing, ...*

c 💬 Discuss the questions.
1 Which of the sports on your lists in 1b have you tried?
2 Which do you think are the most ...?
  - fun
  - exciting
  - dangerous
  - difficult
3 Would you like to try any new sports? Which would you like to try?

2 VOCABULARY Sports

a 💬 Check the meanings of the words in **bold**. Then match the sports in the pictures below with sentences 1–5. Sometimes more than one answer is possible.
1 It's an **extreme** sport.
2 It's a really good **workout**.
3 You win **points** when your opponent **misses** the ball.
4 You usually lose a game if you hit a lot of bad **shots**.
5 The **training** is very difficult.

b ≫ Now go to Vocabulary Focus 10A on p. 142.

table tennis

snowboarding

volleyball

wrestling

diving

a ski jumping

b tennis

c surfing

3 LISTENING

a 💬🔊 Look at the photos below and discuss the questions.

   1 What are these activities? Have you tried them or would you like to?
   2 What do you think is the most fun about them?

b ▶10.02 Listen to Gina and Libby talking about scuba diving and the Color Run. Then answer the questions.

   1 Why do they like each sport?
   2 What do they agree to do at the end?

c 💬🔊 ▶10.02 Listen again and discuss the questions.

   1 Where did Gina try scuba diving?
   2 How much training did she have?
   3 Why was she scared at first?
   4 How long is the run that Libby's going to do?
   5 How is it different from regular runs?

d Which of the two sports sounds more exciting/ dangerous? Which would you rather try? Why?

e 💬🔊 Write down all the reasons why you like your favorite sport. Work with someone who likes a different sport and tell them why you like your favorite.

> Of course, soccer is the greatest game in the world. People in every country love it, and …

4 GRAMMAR Present and future unreal conditionals

a Look at these present and future unreal conditional sentences and <u>underline</u> the correct words to complete the rules.

   • Was it scary? I think if I went, I'd be terrified!
   • If I were in better shape, I would definitely do it.

> 1 We use the present and future unreal conditionals to talk about *things we will probably do in the future / things we imagine, but are not real.*
>
> 2 To form present and future unreal conditionals, we use *If + simple past / simple present, would/will +* base form of the verb.

b ▶10.03 **Pronunciation** Listen to the pronunciation of *would* in each of the sentences. Is it strong (stressed) or weak (not stressed)? Write *S* (strong) or *W* (weak).

   1 If you went, you would absolutely love it.
   2 I wouldn't do a full marathon – I'm not in good enough shape.
   3 It would be more fun if there were a big group of us going.
   4 Would you like to try it?
   5 Yes, I would, but I don't know.
   6 If I were in better shape, I would definitely do it.

c ▶10.03 Listen again and repeat the sentences.

d ≫ Now go to Grammar Focus 10A on p. 162.

e Check (✓) the sentences that are true for you. Then write a present or future unreal conditional sentence for each one saying what you would or might do if things were different.

   ☐ I can't run long distances.
   ☐ I'm not very tall.
   ☐ I don't live in a country that gets a lot of snow.
   ☐ I can't afford a personal fitness trainer.
   ☐ I'm scared of heights.
   ☐ I'm not in good shape.
   ☐ I'm not an Olympic champion.

If I could run long distances, I'd enter a big marathon and raise money for charity.

f 💬🔊 Compare your sentences in 4e.

5 VOCABULARY Adjectives and prepositions

a Some adjectives are followed by a preposition. Complete each sentence with a preposition.

1 I was a little worried _____ it at first.
2 It sounds perfect _____ me!
3 It's popular _____ a lot of different people, not just athletes.

b ▶ 10.05 Listen and check your answers.

c Underline the correct prepositions.

1 ☐ I don't like extreme sports – I'm afraid *about* / *of* hurting myself.
2 ☐ I'm not scared *of* / *to* spiders.
3 ☐ I am very proud *of* / *about* my little sister.
4 ☐ I think that having good friends is essential *of* / *for* a happy, healthy life.
5 ☐ I'm very interested *in* / *about* health and fitness.
6 ☐ I'm worried *of* / *about* my favorite sports team's performance right now.
7 ☐ I'll never get tired *in* / *of* visiting new places.
8 ☐ I've found a sport that is right *for* / *in* me.
9 ☐ I think the quality of women's soccer is similar *to* / *from* men's.

d Check (✓) the sentences in 5c that are true for you. Change the others so that they are true for you.

e Look at ads a–c below. Fill in the blanks with the correct prepositions for the adjectives in bold.

6 SPEAKING

a Write notes about what you would do if you had one of the opportunities below.

learn a new skill or sport
• What would you learn? Why?

take a free trip to anywhere in the world with a friend
• Where would you go? Why?
• Who would you take?

meet a famous person
• Who would you choose?
• What would you say or ask?

travel in time
• What year would you travel to? Why?
• What would you do when you were there?

b 💬 Compare your ideas. Would you like to do the things your partner would like to do?

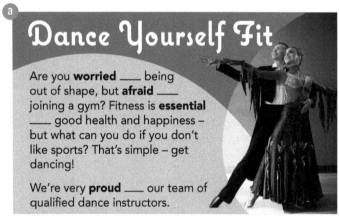

a
Dance Yourself Fit

Are you **worried** ___ being out of shape, but **afraid** ___ joining a gym? Fitness is **essential** ___ good health and happiness – but what can you do if you don't like sports? That's simple – get dancing!

We're very **proud** ___ our team of qualified dance instructors.

b
Become a GUIDE RUNNER

If you want to stay in shape and you're **interested** ___ helping people, too, why not become a guide runner? Running is **popular** ___ blind people, but many of them need a guide runner for support. Just let us know your level of fitness and where you live. You'll even get automatic entry into any races!

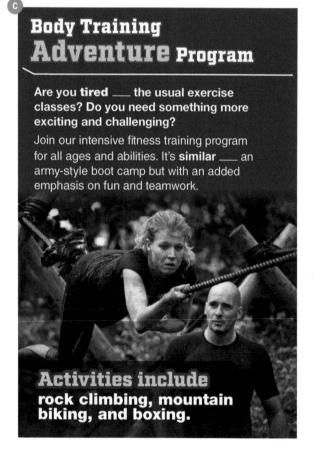

c
Body Training Adventure Program

Are you **tired** ___ the usual exercise classes? Do you need something more exciting and challenging?

Join our intensive fitness training program for all ages and abilities. It's **similar** ___ an army-style boot camp but with an added emphasis on fun and teamwork.

Activities include
rock climbing, mountain biking, and boxing.

10B MAKING THE MOST OF OPPORTUNITIES

1 SPEAKING

a 💬 Discuss the questions.

1 Do you think luck is important in life? Why / Why not?
2 Have you ever had really good or really bad luck? What happened?
3 Can people do anything to make themselves "luckier"? Think of three things.

2 READING

a 💬 Look at the photos, which show details of three true stories about good luck. Can you guess what the three stories might be about?

b 💬 Compare your ideas with other students. Are your ideas the same or different?

JOB SEARCH

FIND JOB

c Read "Searching for Serendipity" quickly. Were your ideas in 2a correct?

Searching *for* Serendipity

HOME | NEWS | YOUR STORIES | LOG IN

Are You Making the Most of Life's Opportunities?

I had my own business but needed a website. My friend Wendy gave me the email address of a designer named Mark. Unfortunately, Wendy's handwriting is awful, so I sent the email to the wrong person. Someone named Matt replied. Obviously, there had been a mistake. He said he wasn't actually a designer – he was a schoolteacher – but he could help me if I wanted!

Matt seemed nice. And anyway, I didn't have anyone else to help me, so I decided to write back to him. In the end, Matt worked on my website for free. He did a great job, and my business started to go really well. Meanwhile, we got to know each other via email. And ten months later, we met. We fell in love immediately, and a year later, we got married. If Wendy had had better handwriting, my business wouldn't have been such a success, and I certainly wouldn't have met Matt!

ANNA

Two years ago, Anna Frances had some very good luck when her colleague gave her some wrong information.

So was Anna just lucky? Or did she make her own luck? Why do these lucky accidents seem to happen to some people and not to others? And is there any way to make yourself more lucky? Well, it seems that the secret of happiness is to make the most of the opportunities that life gives us. We need to be open to serendipity – the random events that lead to happy, sometimes life-changing, results.

Dr. Stephann Makri is working on a project about serendipity at City University, London. He thinks that serendipity is more

than an accident and that we can all have more "luck" if we learn to pay attention to life's opportunities. He has noticed that many people's good-luck stories share the same basic pattern. First, people notice that there is an opportunity. Then they take action to make the most of it. For example, if you imagine meeting an old friend in the street who will later introduce you to the love of your life, several things have to happen. First, you have to notice the friend. Then you have to stop and talk to them, even though you might be busy. Finally, you need to be ready to follow up on whatever comes out of the conversation. So, it might be luck that leads you to walk toward your friend on the street – but the rest is up to you!

More Serendipity Stories ...

TOM

After college, I didn't have a job. I subscribed to a job website and got a lot of emails from them every day. I usually deleted them. One day, I was feeling particularly annoyed by all the emails, so I opened one of them to click on the "unsubscribe" link. But I spotted an interesting job. It was in New York, and I didn't really have the experience they wanted, but I decided to apply. I didn't get the job, but they emailed me two weeks later to say they had another job I could apply for. I got it, and I ended up working in New York City, where I met my girlfriend, Paula. None of it would have happened if I had deleted the email.

CARLA

My mom, Betty, is 71. There's a café in town that I like, and I persuaded my mom to come with me, just to get out of the house. She didn't want to come at first, but when we got there, she really liked the café. While we were there, she started chatting with some bikers. My mom said she had always wanted to ride a motorcycle! I was shocked! Kenny, one of the bikers, offered to take us both out with the rest of the group. To my amazement, my mother said yes! I was really worried, but my mom loved the experience!

d Complete the sentences with the names in the box.

| Anna | Betty | Carla | Kenny | Matt | Tom |

1 _____ failed at first, but was right to take a chance.
2 _____ did an activity she'd always wanted to do.
3 _____ was surprised by someone else's behavior.
4 _____ did some work for someone, even though it wasn't his job.
5 _____ made contact with the wrong person.
6 _____ did something kind for someone the first time they met.

e 💬 Discuss the questions.

1 Which person do you think was the "luckiest"?
2 Do you agree that people make their own luck? Why / Why not?
3 Do you make the most of life's opportunities in a similar way to the people in the stories? Explain your answer.

3 VOCABULARY Expressions with *do*, *make*, and *take*

a Underline the correct answers to complete the summary of Dr. Makri's ideas.

> Can we [1]*take* / *make* / *do* our own luck? Dr. Makri has been [2]*doing* / *making* / *taking* research into serendipity, and he believes we can. The secret lies in [3]*doing* / *taking* / *making* advantage of an opportunity when it comes our way. If you see an opportunity in a chance event, you should [4]*take* / *make* / *do* action and [5]*take* / *have* / *make* the most of that opportunity.
>
> Everyone can be "luckier." If you get out and meet people, you'll have more chance encounters. Be brave and [6]*take* / *make* / *do* risks in order to act freely when an opportunity comes your way.

b ⟫ Now go to Vocabulary Focus 10B on p. 143.

4 GRAMMAR Past unreal conditionals

a Underline the correct words. Then check your answers in the article on p. 120.

If Wendy [1]*had* / *had had* / *would have had* better handwriting, my business [2]*wasn't* / *hadn't been* / *wouldn't have been* such a success, and I certainly [3]*didn't meet* / *hadn't met* / *wouldn't have met* Matt.

b Answer the questions.

1 Did Wendy have good handwriting? Was Anna's business successful? Did she meet Matt?
2 When do we use the past unreal conditional? Choose a or b.
   a to talk about the results of real past events
   b to talk about an imagined past event and its likely result
3 What is the correct form of past unreal conditionals?
   a *If* + simple past, *would* + past participle.
   b *If* + past perfect, *would have* + past participle.

c ▶ 10.06 Listen and match conversations 1–4 with pictures a–d below.

Conversation 1 ☐   Conversation 3 ☐
Conversation 2 ☐   Conversation 4 ☐

d ▶ 10.07 **Pronunciation** Listen to the sentences below. Which words are stressed in each sentence?

1 I would have won easily if I hadn't hurt my arm.
2 I wouldn't have bought it if I'd known it was in such bad condition.
3 If you hadn't pushed me out of the way, that car would have hit me!
4 I wouldn't have discovered the truth if I hadn't read her letters.

e ▶ 10.07 Listen again and practice saying the sentences.

f ⟫ Now go to Grammar Focus 10B on p. 162.

g Write sentences using the past unreal conditional about these people from the article on p. 120.

| Anna | Wendy | Matt | Tom | Betty | Carla | Kenny |

If Anna had used the correct email address, she might not have fallen in love with Matt.

h 💬 Compare your sentences.

5 SPEAKING

a You're going to tell the story of a past event that made your life better. Write notes about one of the topics below.

• a good friend, and how you met them
• a sport or hobby, and how you started doing it
• an accident, and how it happened
• a job, and how you got it
• a school, and why you went there
• a big decision, and how you made it

Think about the important events in your story. What were the consequences of what happened? How would your life have been different if you had done something differently?

b 💬 Take turns telling your stories. Ask each other questions to find out more about what might have happened if things had been different.

What would have been different if you hadn't gone to that school?

I wouldn't have met my best friend, Gabriela.

121

10C EVERYDAY ENGLISH
You have nothing to worry about

1 LISTENING

a  Discuss the questions.

1 When was the last time you were very nervous?
2 What situations make you nervous (e.g., public speaking, flying, starting a new job)? What do you do to calm down?

b ▶ 10.09 Listen to Part 1. What do you think Harry and Noah are talking about?

c ▶ 10.10 Listen to Part 2 to check your answers.

2 USEFUL LANGUAGE
Talking about possible problems and reassuring someone

a ▶ 10.10 Listen to Part 2 again and complete the sentences.

1 You have _____ to worry about.
2 I'm _____ it'll be OK.
3 I'm still _____ that something will go wrong.
4 What _____ she doesn't think I'm right for the job?
5 She's _____ not going to say no.

b Add the sentences in 2a to the chart.

Talking about a problem	Reassuring someone
	You have nothing to worry about.

c 💬 Think of the kinds of worries you might have about these situations. Talk to your partner. Reassure them about their worries.

- doing badly on an exam
- public speaking
- a stressful day at work
- a difficult trip

> I'm worried that I will forget what to say.

> You'll be fine!

3 PRONUNCIATION Sounding sure and unsure

a ▶ 10.11 Listen to this excerpt from the conversation. Does Noah sound sure or unsure?

NOAH Is that a good idea? To ask for a promotion over lunch?

HARRY It would be a more relaxed setting than the office.

b ▶ 10.10 Now listen to Part 2 again. Does Noah sound sure or unsure during the conversation?

c ▶ 10.12 Listen to the following sentences. Do you think the speaker is sure or unsure?

1 **A** Do you think you are prepared for your meeting?
   B I think so, yes.
2 **A** Are you sure you're right for this job?
   B I think so, yes.
3 **A** When will you speak to your boss?
   B Tomorrow at noon.
4 **A** What do you think she will say?
   B Uh, "yes," I think.

4 LISTENING

a 💬🔊 Noah and his boss, Mrs. Grace, are in the restaurant. How do you think Noah feels? What is a good way to ask for a promotion? How would you try to handle this situation?

b ▶10.13 Listen to Part 3. What happens in the meeting? Circle the correct answer.
  1 Noah talks about work because he doesn't want a promotion.
  2 Mrs. Grace offers Noah a promotion before he can ask for one.
  3 Mrs. Grace does not offer Noah a promotion.

c Are the statements true (T) or false (F)?
  1 Noah and Mrs. Grace both think that they went to this restaurant for an interview.
  2 Noah loves his job.
  3 Noah wants to have the office party at the restaurant.
  4 Noah was expecting Mrs. Grace to offer him a promotion.
  5 Noah needs a long time to think about his decision.

5 CONVERSATION SKILLS
Changing the subject

a ▶10.14 Listen and complete the sentences.
  1 **NOAH** That ____ me, though – I need to book this place for the office party next month.
  2 **MRS. GRACE** So, anyway, as I was ____, you've really grown in this job.

b Look again at the sentences in 5a. Who is starting a completely new subject, and who is returning to a previous subject?

c Look at the phrases in **bold**. Are they both ways to change the subject or ways to return to a previous subject?
  1 **Speaking of** cafés, have I told you about the place we found last week?
  2 **By the way,** did you see that new comedy show last night?

d 💬🔊 Work in pairs.
  Student A: You want to talk about your weekend. Talk to Student B. Can you keep the conversation on the same subject?
  Student B: You don't want to hear about Student A's weekend. Try to change the subject and talk about other things (e.g., a movie you've seen recently, someone you saw today, etc.).

> I went to see a movie this weekend.

> Oh, speaking of movies, the latest *Avengers* movie is on TV tonight!

6 SPEAKING

≫ Communication 10C 💬🔊 Student A: Read the information below. Student B: Go to p. 131.

Student A
You want to talk to Student B about a trip abroad you are going to take (where are you going?).
You are worried because:
• you are scared of flying (what might happen?)
• you are nervous about communicating in a different language (what problems might this cause?)
• you are not very good at trying new food (what food might you have to try?).
Write notes, and then have the conversation. Reassure Student B when they try to talk about a big presentation they have to give, but try to bring the conversation back to your trip.

> Anyway, as I was saying, I'm really nervous about what might happen.

> I'm sure you'll do great.

☑ UNIT PROGRESS TEST

→ CHECK YOUR PROGRESS

You can now do the Unit Progress Test.

10D | SKILLS FOR WRITING
I think you should go for it

1 SPEAKING AND READING

a 💬 Read the ad on the right for an organization called NowVolunteer and discuss the questions.

1 What kind of organization do you think NowVolunteer is? What kinds of programs do you think they offer, and where?
2 What kinds of people do you think join a NowVolunteer program, and why?
3 Do you think volunteers have to pay money to work on a program?

b Read the web page below quickly and check your answers to 1a.

⊕ NowVolunteer

Join one of our programs. See the world, help other people, develop new skills.

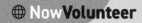

HOME   PROJECTS   JOIN US   ⊕ Now**Volunteer**

Volunteering. Adventure. Experience.

Do you want to have the adventure of a lifetime and make new friends from around the world? NowVolunteer is a volunteer organization that gives young people the opportunity to travel, have fun, and help people.

And we can help your career, too. Companies want to know about your experience, not just about your qualifications. So join us to improve your résumé.

See our volunteer profiles to see what people say about their experiences.

🏅 Unique, award-winning programs

We organize specialized programs in 50 countries. You can work with children, help local communities, work on environmental projects, learn a new skill ... and, at the same time, have a great travel experience.

✉ We arrange everything for you

Just choose a program and we'll take care of the details. All you need to do is raise up to $500 for our programs before you go. We'll provide free accommodations while you're volunteering.

2 LISTENING AND SPEAKING

a You're going to hear Greg talking about his experience with NowVolunteer. Look at the photos below. What do you think he might say about his trip?

Greg from Madison, Wisconsin worked on a community health project in Madagascar.

b ▶ 10.15 Listen to Greg. Does he mention any of your ideas from 2a?

c ▶ 10.15 Listen again and write notes in the chart.

1 What he studied	
2 Reason for going	
3 How he raised money	
4 What he did	
5 What happened next	

d 💬 Discuss the questions.

1 Would you like to join the same program as Greg? Why / Why not?
2 Do you know anyone who has done volunteer work like this? If so, what was their experience like?
3 Have you ever worked for no money? If so, did you enjoy it?

3 READING

a Vicky is in her last year of college, studying marketing. She emailed her friends asking for advice. Read her email and answer the questions.

1 What two programs is Vicky interested in?
2 What might be a problem for her?

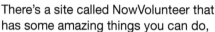
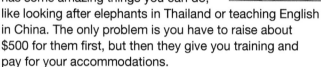

Hi, everyone!

I've been thinking about what to do next year, and I thought I'd take a year off and do some volunteer work.

There's a site called NowVolunteer that has some amazing things you can do, like looking after elephants in Thailand or teaching English in China. The only problem is you have to raise about $500 for them first, but then they give you training and pay for your accommodations.

What do you all think? Am I on to a great idea here, or should I just forget it and start looking around for jobs?

Replies, please! ;-)
Vicky

b ≫ Communication 10D Work in pairs. Student A: Go to p. 130 and read Amanda's reply. Student B: Go to p. 132 and read Laura's reply. Do they think Vicky should do volunteer work? What reasons do they give?

c 💬 Tell your partner about the reply that you read. Who do you agree with?

4 WRITING SKILLS Advising a course of action

a Look at these expressions from the emails Amanda and Laura wrote. Then answer the questions.

1 I think you should …
2 If I were you, I'd …
3 I'm pretty sure you'd …
4 I think you'd have a good time, but …
5 It would definitely …
6 I'm just suggesting that …
7 Maybe it would be better to …

Which expressions … ?

• only give advice
• also imagine what could happen

b Compare Amanda's and Laura's emails. Who uses more "careful" language? Why?

a because she's advising a friend to do something she wants to do
b because she's advising a friend not to do something she wants to do

c Which of these does Laura use?

a adverbs to express uncertainty (*maybe, perhaps*)
b modal verbs to express obligation (*should, must*)
c modal verbs to express uncertainty (*might, could, would*)
d expressions of certainty (*I'm sure, definitely*)
e expressions of uncertainty (*I think, I'm not sure*)

d Rewrite these sentences using the words in parentheses to make the advice more "careful." Make any other changes necessary.

1 Write to them and ask where they spend the money. (If I)
2 Look for a job with a marketing company in Thailand. (better)
3 It won't be very interesting. (not sure)
4 You'll meet a lot of interesting people. (think)
5 Look at the alternatives. (suggesting)

5 WRITING An email with advice

a Think of an alternative to your present lifestyle or job – something you'd like to do for a year. Write an email asking other students if they think it's a good idea.

b Work in pairs. Read your partner's email and write a reply. It can be positive and enthusiastic (like Amanda's) or more careful (like Laura's).

c 💬 Read your partner's reply to your email. Do you think it's good advice? Why / Why not? Does the advice use appropriate expressions?

1 GRAMMAR

Underline the correct words.

1 **A** We lost really badly.
  B I know. We would *scored / have scored* a lot more points if we *did / 'd done* more training over the last few weeks.

2 **A** Are you going to accept the offer?
  B I can't decide. What *would / did* you do if you *were / had been* me?

3 **A** If I *didn't miss / hadn't missed* the train, I'd never *met / have met* my wife, Jasmine.
  B That's so romantic!

4 **A** Hey! Was that a golf ball? Where did it come from?
  B I don't know, but you were very lucky. It *could have / could* hit you!

5 **A** James gets so disappointed when he doesn't win.
  B If he *wasn't / couldn't be* such a competitive person, he wouldn't play as well as he does.

6 **A** Why didn't you call me?
  B Well, I *would / wouldn't* have if I *had / hadn't* left my phone at the office.

2 VOCABULARY

a Complete the sentences with the words in the box.

opponent   of   net   about   point   track   workout

1 It's a fun game and a great _____, too.
2 He'll win the match if he scores one more _____!
3 You won the game! I'm so proud _____ you!
4 You have to hit the ball over the _____.
5 You won last time, but this time your _____ may beat you!
6 How many times did you run around the _____?
7 Are you worried _____ the tennis match tomorrow?

b Complete the questions with the correct form of *make, do,* or *take*.

1 What sports do you _____?
2 Do you know anyone who _____ a lot of risks?
3 How often do you _____ a break when you're studying?
4 Do you _____ the most of your free time? Why / Why not?
5 Should scientists _____ more research into medicine or space travel?
6 Have you ever _____ friends with someone from a different country? Who?
7 Have you ever had to _____ an important decision?

c 💬 Ask and answer the questions in 2b.

3 WORDPOWER Easily confused words

a Match the sentence halves.

1 ☐ If you need money,   a I can **lend** you some.
2 ☐ I need some money,   b so I'll have to **borrow** some.

3 ☐ Go on! Don't **miss**   a points if you run with the ball.
4 ☐ You'll **lose**   b this opportunity! It'll change your life!

5 ☐ **Take** some water   a when you come to the gym.
6 ☐ **Bring** some energy drinks b when you go running.

7 ☐ If you want to take part, a **raise** your hand.
8 ☐ If you have work experience, b your chances of getting a job will **rise**.

9 ☐ They **robbed**   a the money from a bank.
10 ☐ They **stole**   b a bank.

11 ☐ Where are you working? a I'm **currently** working at home.
12 ☐ Do you work at a bank?   b **Actually**, I work at a school.

b Underline the correct words.

1 a borrow = *take / give*
  b lend = *take / give*
2 a miss = *not win / not take*
  b lose = *not win / not take*
3 a take = *to here / away from here*
  b bring = *to here / away from here*
4 a raise = *lift something / go up*
  b rise = *lift something / go up*
5 a rob = *take from a person or place / take something*
  b steal = *take from a person or place / take something*
6 a currently = *at the moment / in fact*
  b actually = *at the moment / in fact*

c Write down three ...
  • places that can be robbed.
  • things that are difficult to steal.
  • things that you would only lend to a good friend.
  • things you sometimes borrow.
  • things you always take with you when you go out.
  • things people often bring back from vacation.

d 💬 Compare your answers for c. Are they the same or different?

⟳ REVIEW YOUR PROGRESS

How well did you do in this unit? Write 3, 2, or 1 for each objective.
3 = very well   2 = well   1 = not so well

I CAN ...	
talk about new things it would be good to do	☐
talk about imagined past events	☐
talk about possible problems and reassure someone	☐
write an email with advice.	☐

This page is intentionally left blank.

COMMUNICATION PLUS

6A VOCABULARY Student A

1 Read definitions 1–5 aloud. Student B will match them to compound nouns. Look at the answers in parentheses. Tell Student B if their answers are correct.

1 something you need in order to get on a plane (boarding pass)
2 a place you go to stay in a tent (campground)
3 a machine for keeping your room cool (air conditioner)
4 a guided visit to the famous places in a town or city (sightseeing tour)
5 a machine that washes your plates, glasses, knives and forks, etc. (dishwasher)

2 Listen to Student B's definitions. Find matching compound nouns in the box. Choose one word from each column.

street	control
window	bag
bottle	map
passport	opener
sleeping	seat

⋙ Now go back to p. 69.

10D READING Student A

✉ ✐ ☆ ⚐   ⊗

Hi Vicky,

No wonder you don't want to go straight into an office job next year. Looking after elephants in Thailand sounds much more exciting! I think you should definitely go for it. You don't have much to lose (except a little money), and if it doesn't work out, you can always come back. But anyway, I'm pretty sure you'd enjoy it and have a great time – you have always been good with animals. It would definitely look good on your résumé, too. It would show that you're an adventurous person and you're interested in different things, not just studying and jobs. Too bad I've got a job already or I'd come with you! ;-)

Let me know what you decide.

Love,
Amanda

⋙ Now go back to p. 125.

6C SPEAKING Student B

1 Your partner will tell you some surprising news. Listen to the news and give some recommendations.
2 You found an old ring in your house. You think it belonged to your great-grandmother, but you aren't sure. You cleaned it and showed it to a friend, who said it was very valuable. Your friend said you could sell it for about $1,000,000. Tell your partner your news, and ask for some recommendations about what to do.

⋙ Now go back to p. 75.

8B SPEAKING AND READING

⋙ Now go back to p. 95.

9A GRAMMAR Student B

Audio streaming facts and figures
Audio *has streamed / has been streamed* in the U.S. since
1993. It *started / was started* by an organization called the
Internet Underground Music Archive. Now the most popular
streaming services that fans *use / are used* are Spotify,
Pandora, and Apple. The music industry worldwide *has
taken / has been taken* over by digital streaming. More than
54% of music sales *come / is come* from streaming.

⋙ Now go back to p. 106.

9C SPEAKING Student B

You want to arrange an afternoon with Student A.
* You don't really like modern art.
* You are hungry. You've heard about a new café
  that has good food and great coffee. You can't
  remember what it is called, but you have the
  details on your phone.
* There is an exhibition of photography across town,
  but you don't know where.

⋙ Now go back to p. 111.

10C SPEAKING Student B

You want to talk to Student A about a big presentation
you have to do (where? what is it about?).
You're worried because:
* you don't have much time to prepare (when is it?)
* you don't have any experience with public speaking
  (what problems might you have?)
* you are worried people might ask difficult
  questions (what might they ask?).
Write notes. Then have the conversation. Reassure
Student A about the trip they are going on, but try to
bring the conversation back to your presentation.

⋙ Now go back to p. 123.

6A VOCABULARY Student B

1 Listen to Student A's definitions. Find matching compound nouns in the box. Choose one word from each column.

boarding	washer
camp	conditioner
air	tour
sightseeing	ground
dish	pass

2 Read definitions 1–5 aloud. Student A will match them to compound nouns. Look at the answers in parentheses. Tell Student A if their answers are correct.

1 a plan that shows where things are in a town or city (street map)
2 a place to sit on a plane or train where you can easily look outside (window seat)
3 a gadget for taking the tops off glass bottles (bottle opener)
4 a place where you have to show your identification at an airport (passport control)
5 something you use to keep warm at night when you go camping (sleeping bag)

》》 Now go back to p. 69.

10D READING Student B

⊠ ☑ ☆ ⼝   ⊗

Hi Vicky,

I'm not sure what I think about your idea of doing a year abroad. I can see that it might be exciting to go off to somewhere like Thailand or China for a year, but if I were you, I'd think very carefully about it before you make a decision.

I think you'd have a good time, but you also need to think about getting a job after you come back. While you're away in Thailand, everyone else will be looking for jobs. Maybe it would be better to do something more closely connected with marketing. I'm not sure experience with elephants would help much in getting you a marketing job!

Anyway, I don't want to sound negative, but I'm just suggesting that you think about it first and make sure it's what you really want to do.

We could meet up and talk about it if you like.

Love,
Laura

》》 Now go back to p. 125.

7C SPEAKING Student B

1 Student A is staying in your home. They will ask you for permission to do things. Decide whether or not to give permission.

2 You have started a new job, and Student A is your coworker. Ask permission to:
• play music at your desk while you're working
• turn the air conditioning up
• move your desk closer to the window.

》》 Now go back to p. 87.

VOCABULARY FOCUS

6B Describing food

a ▶06.07 Label the pictures using the pairs of adjectives in the box. Then listen and check.

creamy / crunchy   fresh / dried   cooked / raw
heavy / light   sweet / sour

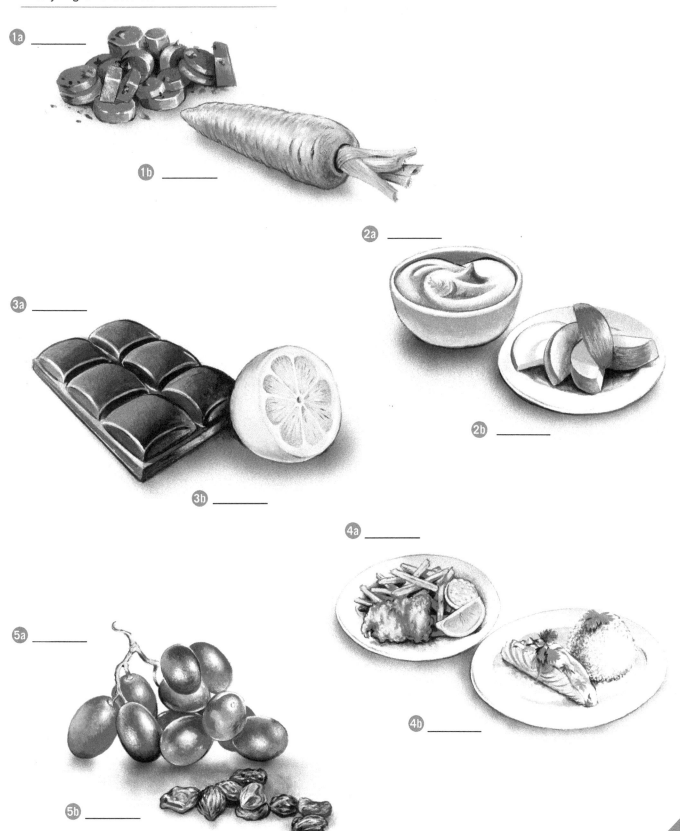

1a _____

1b _____

2a _____

2b _____

3a _____

3b _____

4a _____

4b _____

5a _____

5b _____

b Complete the two recipes with the words in the boxes.

mash squeeze chop serve mix

Guacamole

1 _____ three chilies, three tomatoes, one onion, and a bunch of cilantro.

2 _____ three avocados in a bowl.

3 _____ all the ingredients together.

4 _____ the juice of half a lime into the mixture.

5 _____ with tortilla chips.

stir chop fry add heat up

MEATBALLS
IN TOMATO SAUCE

1 _____ one onion and two cloves of garlic.

2 _____ 500 g minced lamb to the onions and garlic, with salt, pepper, and spices. Make the mixture into balls.

3 _____ one tablespoon of olive oil in a pan.

4 _____ the meatballs in the oil.

5 Add two cans of tomatoes and 200 ml of water. Cook for 30 minutes. _____ occasionally.

c Prepare a simple recipe for a dish you like. Write notes about the ingredients you need and how you make it.

d 💬 Take turns talking about your recipes. Would you like to eat each other's dishes?

e ≫ Now go back to p. 71.

7A Describing houses and buildings

a ▶ 07.06 Use the words in the box to label the pictures. Then listen and check.

attic   balcony   basement   apartment building   doorbell   second floor
front door   first floor   landing   lock   steps   window

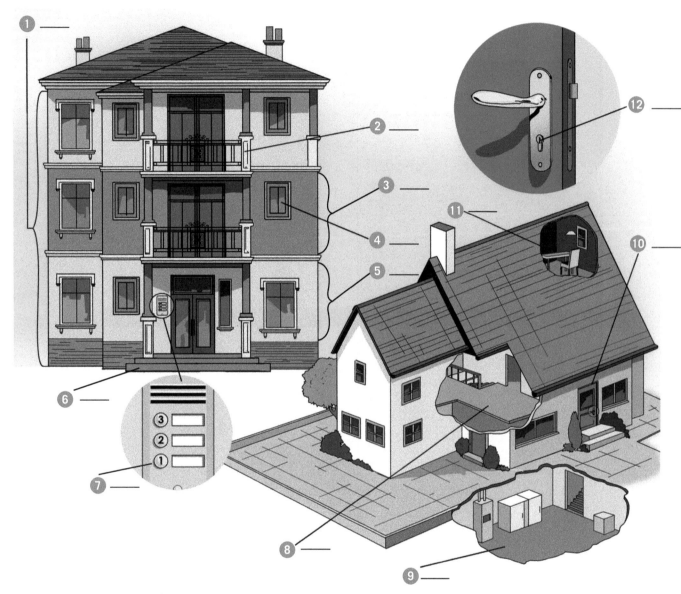

b ▶ 07.07 Complete the sentences with the words in the box. Then listen and check.

attic   balcony   floor   location   moved
neighborhood   rent   view

1 I don't own my own house, so I _____ the house I'm living in.
2 I've _____ a lot of times, so I've had a lot of different addresses.
3 I live in a very busy _____. There are a lot of stores, cafés, and cars.
4 We don't have a yard, but we do have a _____ where we can sit outside.
5 My home is in a good _____ because it's near the train station.
6 I put all the stuff I don't use in the _____.
7 Our apartment is on the third _____ of our building.
8 The _____ from my bedroom is nothing special – just a street and more houses.

c 💬 Discuss the sentences in **b** that are true for you.

The second sentence isn't true for me. I've only moved once in my life.

d 💬 Imagine you are going to buy or rent a new home. What kind of house or apartment would you choose and why? Which of these things are most important to you?
- price
- views
- location
- number of rooms
- yard
- something else

e ≫ Now turn to p. 81.

8A Sharing information

a   Underline the correct verb in the examples. Check (✓) the examples where both verbs collocate with the noun.

1   *create / make* a podcast
2   *send / post* a text or email
3   *put up / deliver* a poster
4   *send / post* on social media

5   *have / hold* a chat or talk with someone
6   *deliver / send* a flyer
7   *create / hold* a meeting
8   *make / brainstorm* ideas

b   Put the collocations in the chart below. Some can go in more than one category.

Involves talking	Involves writing

Involves technology	Doesn't need to involve technology

c   Read sentences 1–3. Match the words in **bold** to definitions a–f.

1   I **subscribe** to podcasts on a lot of different topics – sports, music, politics, and cooking.
2   I found a new **series** of comedy podcasts – each **episode** is absolutely hilarious.
3   I subscribe to this news podcast that's like a kind of **newsfeed** – **items** are **updated** every hour.

a   regular delivery of the latest news
b   one single podcast from a group of connected podcasts
c   to choose to receive new podcasts from someone who creates them on a regular basis
d   a number of related podcasts that follow one another
e   replaced with newer ones
f   individual pieces of news

d   💬 Discuss the questions.

1   What are popular topics for podcasts in your country?
2   If you subscribe to any podcasts, what are they about?
    If you don't listen to podcasts, what kind do you think could be interesting?
3   How do most people in your country get news – from the radio, TV, social media, or podcasts?

e   ≫ Now go back to p. 92.

8B Reporting verbs

a Match the statements with the pictures a–f. Where are the people and what are they doing?

1 "I'll pay for lunch if you like." _____
2 "OK, it's true. I wrote all the reviews." _____
3 "Don't sit down!" _____
4 "Don't forget to read the label." _____
5 "Why don't we ask someone for directions?" _____
6 "If I were you, I'd make a formal complaint." _____

b 💬 Write what happened in the situations in **a** using the verbs in the box. Then compare your answers with other students.

admitted	advised	~~offered~~	reminded	suggested	warned

> We were in a restaurant, and he **offered** to pay for lunch.

c 💬 Work with a partner. Student A: Look at the sentences in **a** and write one sentence like these in direct speech. Then read it aloud to your partner. Student B: Summarize what A said using a reporting verb from **b**.

> Don't tell the boss!

> You warned me not to tell the boss.

d ≫ Now go back to p. 97.

10A Sports

a ▶ 10.01 Label the pictures with the words in the box. Then listen and check.

competitor   court   net   opponents   referee   track

1 _____

2 _____

3 _____

4 _____

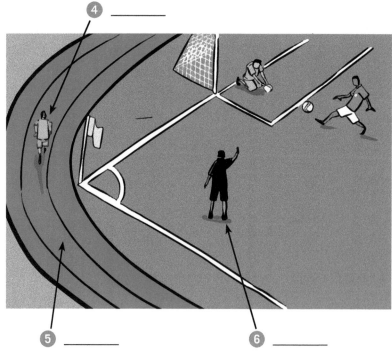

5 _____

6 _____

b <u>Underline</u> the word in each group that is <u>not</u> possible.
You can …
1 *win / lose / beat / score* a point.
2 *beat / attack / score* your opponent.
3 win a *game / point / match / competitor.*
4 *compete for / win / score* a prize.

c 💬 Discuss the questions.
1 When did you last play a game or a sports match? What happened? Did you win?
2 Do you prefer playing on a team or individually?
3 Are you a competitive person?

d Think of a sport and write notes on these questions.
1 Is it a team sport or an individual sport?
2 How do you play it?
3 Do you need a special place or special equipment?
4 Are there any special rules?
5 Is it a popular sport?

e 💬 Describe your sport but do <u>not</u> say its name. Try to guess your partner's sport.

f ≫ Now turn to p. 117.

10B Expressions with *do, make,* and *take*

a Write *do, make,* or *take* for each group of words.
1 _____ money, a decision, a mistake, progress
2 _____ a risk, advantage of something, a chance
3 _____ sense, a difference, the most of something
4 _____ your homework, (some) research
5 _____ well/badly (e.g., on an exam), your best
6 _____ part in something, care of someone, action
7 _____ a break, a nap, it easy
8 _____ a phone call, new friends easily

b Complete questions 1–6 using words from **a** or your own ideas.
When was the last time you … ?
1 took _____   4 did _____
2 made _____   5 did _____
3 took _____   6 made _____

c  Ask and answer the questions in **b**.

d ≫ Now go back to p. 121.

GRAMMAR FOCUS

6A Modals of obligation

 06.04 *must, have to,* and *need to*

We use *have to* or *need to* to say something is necessary:
You **have to buy** *a ticket before you get on the train.*
We **need to** *show our tickets on the train.*
Must is very strong and can be formal or official. We often see *must* in written rules or laws. It is not common in speaking.
Employees **must** *wash their hands.*
There is no past or future form of *must*. When we talk about rules in the past or future, we always use the correct form of *have to* or *need to*:
*When you go to India, you***'ll need to** *get a visa.*
I **had to** *wear a uniform at school.*

> 🗨 **Tip**
>
> Don't use contractions with *have to*:
> *I have to go.* NOT ~~I've to go.~~

> 🗨 **Tip**
>
> • Often there is not much difference in meaning between *need to* and *have to*.
> • *Have got to* is also used in spoken English and means the same as *have to*.
> • Questions with *must* are very rare.

 06.05 *must not, can't,* and *don't have to*

We use *must not* or *can't* to say that something is not allowed. *Can't* is much more common in spoken English. We use *must not* to express strong prohibition or to say something is forbidden.
Drivers **must not** *text and drive.*
We **can't** *cross the road yet – the light's still red.*
For things that were not allowed in the past, use *couldn't*:
I **couldn't** *work in Peru because I only had a tourist visa.*

We use *don't have to* or *don't need to* when there is no obligation. It means it is not necessary to do something:
College students **don't have to wear** *a uniform.*
I **didn't need to** *call a taxi. Robert drove me home.*

▶ **06.06** *should* and *ought to*
We use *should* or *ought to* to give advice and recommendations. They have the same meaning, but *ought to* is rarely used in the negative. We use *shouldn't* instead:
We **should see** *as much as possible. We* **shouldn't waste** *time.*
We **ought to see** *as much as possible.*

Next we need to make the sandwiches. We don't have to make a cake because Francesca bought one.

6B Comparatives and superlatives

	Adjectives		Adverbs
One syllable	*rich → rich**er**, **the** rich**est***		*fast → fast**er**, **the** fast**est***
Two or more syllables*	**Ending in -*y*:** *easy → eas**ier**, **the** eas**iest*** *friendly → friendl**ier**, the friendl**iest***		**All:** *often → **more** often, **the** **most** often* *carefully →* **more** *carefully,* **the most** *carefully*
	Other: *careful → **more** careful, **the** **most** careful*		
Exceptions	*good → **better, the best*** *bad → **worse, the worst*** *far → **farther, the farthest*** **more** / **the most** *bored / tired*		*well → **better, the best*** *badly → **worse, the worst*** *far → **farther, the farthest*** *early → **earlier, the earliest***

*Some two-syllable adjectives can follow the rules for one-syllable adjectives: *narrow, shallow, quiet, simple.*

▶ **06.11** Comparison
We can use comparative adjectives and adverbs to compare two things, situations, times, actions, etc., usually with *than*. We can change the degree of comparison with words like *a lot, much, far, even, slightly, a little*:
Life's **a lot more interesting than** *before.*
She's **a little happier than** *she used to be.*
He's speaking **much more slowly than** *usual today.*

The opposite of *more* is *less*. We can use it with all adjectives and adverbs:
The car's **slightly less clean than** *it was.*
I walk **less quickly than** *he does.*

as + adjective/adverb + *as* shows that two things are equal; *not as … as* means *less than*:
They're **as wealthy as** *some Hollywood actors.*
She doesn't **listen as carefully as** *she should.*

Some common adverbs can change the degree of the comparison:
You're **just** *as pretty as your sister!* (= exactly equal)
My brother isn't **nearly** *as hard-working as me.*
(= very different)
She doesn't sing **quite** *as well as I do.*
(= slightly different)

Extremes
We use superlative adjectives and adverbs to talk about extremes:
It's **the worst** *hotel in the world!*
I got **the lowest** *score possible.*

We often use the present perfect with *ever* with superlatives:
This is **the best** *meal I***'ve ever eaten**.
It was **the least interesting** *movie I***'ve ever seen**.

We can use the expression *by far* to say an extreme is very different from all others:
That's **by far the highest** *mountain I've ever climbed.*

6A Modals of obligation

a   Complete the sentences with the correct form of *have to, need to,* or *must*. Sometimes more than one answer is possible.

1   In my country, you ____have to____ (have to / need to) cross the road at a crosswalk – it's illegal to cross anywhere else.
2   When I lived in Moscow, I _____ (need to / must) leave home two hours before work because the rush hour traffic was so bad.
3   _____ Alex _____ (have to / must) wear a tie to work?
4   I'll tell you a secret, but you _____ (have to / must) tell anyone. I don't want anyone else to know.
5   We took plenty of money, but in the end, we _____ (have to / must) pay – everything was free.
6   All visitors _____ (have to / must) report to reception.
7   If you want to be there on time, you'll _____ (have to / need to) leave here very soon.
8   Your brother can borrow my books tonight, but he _____ (need to / must) forget to bring them back tomorrow. I need them for my class in the morning.

b   Look at the signs. Then complete the advice using the verbs in parentheses and a modal verb. Sometimes more than one form is possible.

You ¹ _must not / can't park_ (park) here.

You ² _____ (pay) for the bus to the shopping mall.

You ³ _____ (leave) your car unlocked. It might get stolen.

You ⁴ _____ (use) that door – it's for emergencies only.

You ⁵ _____ (only use) the official taxis.

c   ≫ Now go back to p. 70.

6B Comparatives and superlatives

a   Complete the sentences with the comparative or superlative form of the words in parentheses. Add *than* or *the* where necessary.

1   Indian food is ____spicier than____ French food. (spicy)
2   This is _____ meal I've ever eaten. (delicious)
3   The weather was _____ I expected. (hot)
4   She's a _____ driver _____ I am. (slow)
5   Are you _____ person in your class? (smart)
6   I didn't have a good vacation. The _____ thing was the hotel. It was terrible. (bad)
7   Your English is _____ mine. (good)
8   I'm sorry, I can't come on Friday. That's my _____ day. (busy)

b   Complete the sentences so that they mean the same as the sentences in **a**. Use two to five words.

1   French food isn't ____as spicy as Indian food____.
2   I've never eaten a _____ meal than this.
3   I didn't expect the weather to be _____ it was.
4   She drives _____ I do.
5   Is anybody in your class _____ you?
6   I didn't have a good vacation. The hotel was _____ everything else.
7   I don't speak English _____ you do.
8   I'm sorry, I can't come on Friday. It's _____ the other days.

c   Complete the sentences with one word from the box in each space. Use each word once only.

| ~~a~~ | as | little | by | ever | just | ~~more~~ |
| most | nearly | one | slightly | than | the |

1   Today's lesson was ____a____ lot ____more____ interesting than usual – it was excellent.
2   That's _____ worst joke I've _____ heard!
3   The exam went really well. It wasn't _____ as difficult as I expected.
4   I think she's _____ of the _____ innovative designers in the world.
5   Our vacation was a _____ more expensive _____ we thought, but it was still a good value.
6   They started _____ later than usual, but they still finished on time.
7   _____ far the oldest person in my family is my great-grandmother.
8   Our new TV is fantastic – the picture quality is _____ as good _____ in the movie theater, or maybe even better.

d   ≫ Now go back to p. 72.

7A Modals of deduction

We can use modal verbs to show that we are making a deduction using evidence, not stating a fact:

▶ 07.03

We **must be** early. Nobody else has arrived yet.
They work at the same office, so they **may know** each other.
She **might not be** in. The lights are all out.
That **can't be** Mark's car. He told me it was in the garage.

Different modal verbs tell us how sure about a deduction we are:

It's cold in that house.	Fact: I **know** it is.
It **must** be cold in that house.	Deduction: I'm **sure** it is.
It **may / might / could** be cold in that house.	Deduction: It's **possible** that it is.
It **may / might** not be cold in that house.	Deduction: It's **possible** that it isn't.
It **can't** be cold in that house.	Deduction: I'm **sure** it isn't.
It isn't cold in that house.	Fact: I know it isn't.

- The opposite of *must* for deductions is *can't*. Don't use *must not, can,* or *couldn't* for deductions:
  This bill **can't** be right. I only ordered a salad.
  NOT ~~This bill couldn't / must not be right.~~
  There **must** be a mistake.
  NOT ~~There can be a mistake.~~
- There is almost no difference between *may, might,* and *could*. All three mean that something is possible.
- To make deductions about actions happening now, use a modal + *be* + verb + *-ing*:
  She isn't answering the phone. She **might be listening** to music.

7B Quantifiers

▶ 07.10 *some, any,* and *no*

We usually use *some* in affirmative statements and in questions that are offers. We use *any* in negative statements and other questions:
There are **some** nice views from the hotel.
Would you like **some** coffee?
He doesn**'t** have **any** good music.
Do you have **any** local currency?

We can use *no* in affirmative sentences to talk about zero quantity:
There's **no** crime around here.

To talk about zero quantity, we can also use *none of* + plural / noncount or *none*:
None of my friends could help.
A How many vacations have you taken this year?
B **None** at all.

▶ 07.11 Large quantities

We use *lots of / a lot of* in affirmative sentences, *not many / not much / not a lot of* in negative sentences, and *many / much / a lot of* in questions:
There are **a lot of** cars on the road today.
I don**'t** have **much** money with me.
Did **many** people come to the concert?
We don**'t** need **a lot of** time to finish this work.

In affirmative sentences, we can use *plenty of* to show we are happy with the amount:
Don't worry – we have **plenty of** food.

▶ 07.12 Small quantities

We use *a few / a little* to talk about an amount. We use *few / little* to talk about a negative amount (i.e., there is not a lot):
We have **a little** time before the show starts.
I need **a few** things from the store.
I have **very little** time to finish this work.
This dish has **very few** ingredients.

We can say *quite a few / very few / very little* to increase / decrease the amount.

▶ 07.13 *too / not enough*

We use *too much / too many* + noun to say there is more than the right amount. We use *not enough* to say there is less than the right amount:
I have **too much furniture**. There is**n't enough room** for all of it!
I couldn't move at the concert because there were **too many people**.

We also use *too* + adjective / adverb and *not* + adjective / adverb *enough*:
This suitcase is **too heavy**. They won't let you take it on the plane.
You're walking **too quickly**. I can't keep up!
The meeting room is**n't big enough** for all of us. There are**n't enough** chairs.
You're **not** walking **fast enough**. Hurry up!

> Tip
>
> We use *few* with count nouns. We use *little* with noncount nouns.
> **a few** friends / **a little** money
> We use *(too) many* with plural count nouns. We use *(too) much* with noncount nouns.
> **too many** potatoes / **too much** soda

7A Modals of deduction

a Match the deductions 1–8 with the best sentences a–h.

1. [f] That man must be a doctor.
2. [ ] That man might be a doctor.
3. [ ] That man might not be a doctor.
4. [ ] That man can't be a doctor.
5. [ ] They must be eating dinner now.
6. [ ] They could be eating dinner now.
7. [ ] They may not be eating dinner now.
8. [ ] They can't be eating dinner now.

a He doesn't know anything about medicine.
b They finished their dinner an hour ago.
c He's wearing a white coat.
d I remember they booked a table at a restaurant for this time.
e Perhaps they've finished.
f Look – he's listening to that man's heart.
g They usually eat around this time.
h It's possible that he's a nurse.

b Complete the sentences using an appropriate modal of deduction. Sometimes more than one modal is possible.

1. It's impossible that she's in the office – she flew to Beijing yesterday.
   She _can't be in the office – she flew to Beijing yesterday._
2. I'm sure you're right.
   You _____
3. It's possible that they want to sell their apartment.
   They _____
4. I'm sure he isn't speaking Russian – it sounds more like Spanish to me.
   He _____ – it sounds more like Spanish to me.
5. It's possible that you're the perfect person for the job.
   You _____
6. There's a possibility that he doesn't know the answer.
   He _____
7. I'm sure you don't need that coat today – it's 30 degrees!
   It's 30 degrees! You _____
8. They're probably building a new shopping center.
   They _____

c ⟫ Now go back to p. 80.

7B Quantifiers

a Underline the correct quantifier in each sentence.

1. We had *any* / <u>*no*</u> / *none* problems.
2. My parents read *a lot* / *a lot of* / *much* books.
3. I'm not tall *enough* / *too* / *plenty* to be a police officer.
4. There's too *little* / *many* / *much* noise in my neighborhood. I can't sleep.
5. You don't go out *little* / *many* / *enough*. You should go out more.
6. I watch *much* / *many* / *a lot of* television.
7. **A** Did you get much work done?
   B Yes, I got *a lot of* / *a lot* / *none* done.
8. **A** Do you have any potatoes?
   B No, I don't have *some* / *any* / *none*.
9. I've been to quite *many* / *few* / *a few* countries.
10. It's *too much* / *too* / *enough* hot in here. Can I open a window?

b Complete the second sentence so that it means the same as the first sentence.

1. **a** I want no visitors for the next 30 minutes.
   b I don't _want any visitors for the next 30 minutes._
2. **a** There aren't enough chairs for everyone.
   b There are too _____
3. **a** I wanted a cookie, but there weren't any left.
   b I wanted a cookie, but there were _____
4. **a** Make sure you take plenty of money.
   b Make sure you take a _____
5. **a** They gave us too little information.
   b They didn't _____
6. **a** I didn't see many people.
   b I saw very _____
7. **a** We didn't have any money.
   b We had _____
8. **a** She has plenty of time tomorrow.
   b She has a _____

c ⟫ Now go back to p. 85.

8A Reported speech

Reported speech and direct speech
When we talk about what somebody said or thought, we can use direct speech or reported speech:

* *Direct speech:* He said, "I don't want to talk to you."
* *Reported speech:* He said he didn't want to talk to me.

 08.04

Direct speech	Reported speech
"I **don't want** to talk to you." →	He said he **didn't want** to talk to me.
"I'm **planning** to resign." →	She said she **was planning** to resign.
"I've already **told** you." →	He said **he had** already **told** me.
"I **saw** you break it." →	I told him I **had seen** him break it.
"I'm **going to cook** tonight." →	You said you **were going to cook** tonight.
"I'**ll** see you soon." →	He said he **would** see me soon.
"I **can't** hear you." →	She said she **could**n't hear me.
"You **may** be right." →	He said I **might** be right.

Some modal verbs (*would, could, should, might*) stay the same in reported speech:

I'**d** like to go. → He said he'**d** like to go.
It **might** be difficult → She said it **might** be difficult.

08.05 Reported questions
When you report a *Wh-* question, put the subject before the verb. Don't use the auxiliary *do / does / did*:

"Where **are you** from?" → She asked me where **I was** from.
"Why **did she say** that?" → He asked me why **she had said** that.

For *Yes/No* questions, use *if/whether*. *Whether* is more formal than *if*:

"Are you going to help?" → We asked them **if** they were going to help.
"Did you visit the London Eye?" → She asked us **whether** we had visited the London Eye.

Other changes
When we report speech, we usually need to change the pronouns (e.g., *I*, *he*) and possessives (e.g., *my*), depending on who is talking to whom. Time and place words may also need to change:

"**I** want **you** to give **this** message to **your** boss **tonight**."
→ She said **she** wanted **me** to give **a / the** message to **my** boss **that night**.

> 💬 **Tip**
>
> You don't need to change the tense when you want to show that the speaker's words are still true now:
> I **told** you yesterday that I **don't** want to talk to you.
> (= I still don't want to talk to you today.)

Say and *tell* have different patterns. Always use a person or pronoun after *tell*:

Tom **said** he had a new car. NOT ~~Tom said me he had a new car.~~
Tom **told me** he had a new car. NOT ~~Tom told he had a new car.~~

8B Verb patterns

08.06 verb + *-ing* or infinitive
* Some verbs (e.g., *enjoy, mind, keep, admit, recommend, suggest*) are followed by a verb + *-ing*:
  She **didn't mind working** late.
  The negative form is *not* + verb + *-ing*:
  I **enjoyed not cooking** for a change.
* Other verbs (e.g., *want, hope, agree, offer, promise, refuse, threaten, plan*) are followed by an infinitive:
  They **threatened to tell** the police.
  The negative form is *not* + infinitive:
  I **promise not to break** anything.
* Some verbs (e.g., *start, begin, continue*) can be followed by both patterns, with no change of meaning:
  People **started arriving** an hour ago.
  He **started to feel** angry.
* Some verbs (e.g., *try, forget, remember*) can be followed by both patterns, but the meaning changes:
  I **tried reading** some reviews online, but they didn't help much. (= I read them as an experiment)
  I **tried to read** some reviews online, but my Internet connection wasn't working. (= I attempted to read them)
  I **remember going** there for the first time. (= I'm looking back at an earlier experience)
  Please **remember to book** a table. (= keep the plan in your memory)

* Some verbs (e.g., *advise, ask, invite, remind, tell, warn*) need an object before the infinitive:
  They **warned** me not **to tell** anyone.
  I've **invited** your parents **to visit** us.
  Make (= force) and *let* (= allow) are followed by an object and the base form:
  My boss **made me work** late.
  He **let me drive** his car.

Other uses of verb + *-ing*
* When a verb comes after a preposition (e.g., *about, of, by*), the verb is always in the *-ing* form:
  I'm worried **about** not be**ing** good enough.
  They escaped **by** break**ing** a window.
* When a verb is the subject of a sentence, it is usually in the *-ing* form:
  Eating in a restaurant is more expensive than eating at home.

Other uses of the infinitive
* Infinitive of purpose:
  I went online **to read** the news.
* adjective + infinitive:
  I was relieved **to see** I wasn't late.
* verb + question word + infinitive:
  I don't know where **to go** or who **to ask**.

8A Reported speech

a Complete the reported speech with the correct verb form. Change the tense where possible.

1 "It's going to be a beautiful day."   He said it ____was going to be____ a beautiful day.
2 "I don't want to go out this evening."   She told me she _____ that evening.
3 "We're waiting for you."   They said they _____ for us.
4 "My sister can't drive."   She said her sister _____.
5 "I've lost my car keys."   She told me she _____ her car keys.
6 "Lucy might have a new job."   He said Lucy _____ a new job.
7 "I'll help you with those bags."   He said he _____ me with my bags.
8 "Mark bought a new car."   You told me that Mark _____ a new car.

b Read Harry's conversation with Andy. Then choose the best word or phrase to complete Andy's conversation with Harry's sister, Lucy.

> **HARRY** I'm trying to buy a book for my sister, Lucy. It's her birthday tomorrow.
> **ANDY** What kinds of books does she like?
> **HARRY** I'm not sure. She likes reading about history.
> **ANDY** This is really good, *A Short History of the World*. I read it a few months ago.
> **HARRY** No, I think she's already read that. She didn't like it. No, I'm going to get her this one, *A History of Amazing Buildings*. I think she'll love it.
>
> *Two days later, Andy sees Lucy in the street …*
>
> **ANDY** Hi, Lucy. I saw your brother a few days ago – he said it was ¹*my / your / her* birthday ²*tomorrow / the previous day / yesterday*.
> **LUCY** Yes, that's right. Where did you see him?
> **ANDY** At the bookstore. When I asked him what he was doing ³*here / there / near*, he said ⁴*he was / he's / I'm* looking for a present for ⁵*me / you / her*.
> **LUCY** Really?
> **ANDY** Yes. I asked him what books ⁶*you liked / do you like / does she like*, and he said he wasn't sure. He said ⁷*she reads / you read / I read* history books. So I showed him *A Short History of the World* – I said it was really good. I told him ⁸*you've / I've / I'd* read it a few months ⁹*earlier / ago / later*. But he said ¹⁰*you'd / she's / I'd* already read it, and you hadn't liked it.
> **LUCY** What? I thought it was wonderful!
> **ANDY** Yeah. Anyway, he said ¹¹*I'm / he's / he was* going to get *A History of Amazing Buildings*.
> **LUCY** Yes – and he did. It's really cool.
> **ANDY** Great – he said ¹²*you'd love it / she'll love that / you'll love that*.

c ⟫ Now go back to p. 94.

8B Verb patterns

a Underline the correct option.

1 I agreed *going / to go* to the hospital.
2 He admitted *to take / taking* the money.
3 Remember *to pick up / picking up* the dry cleaning on your way home.
4 We tried *making / to make* a cake, but the oven wasn't working.
5 I made the dog *sit / sitting* down.
6 Maria refused *watching / to watch* the scary movie.
7 It's important *making / to make* a reservation in advance.
8 They don't mind *walking / to walk* home tonight.
9 We advised *to take / them to take* a short vacation.
10 When I was a kid, my mom always let me *stay / to stay* up late.

b Complete the conversation.

A I want ¹ ___to get___ (get) my laptop fixed. I don't know where ² _____ (go).
B Have you tried ³ _____ (look) online? It's easy ⁴ _____ (find) repair shops, and you can read reviews ⁵ _____ (see) if they're good.
A Uh … no. ⁶ _____ (check) the Internet is going to be pretty difficult because my computer's broken.
B Oh, right, sorry, I keep ⁷ _____ (forget). Listen, I think I know who ⁸ _____ (ask). My neighbor's a computer engineer. I'll call him now ⁹ _____ (ask) him what ¹⁰ _____ (do).

Five minutes later …

B OK, so he says he doesn't mind ¹¹ _____ (help), but he's a little busy. He suggests ¹² _____ (turn) it off and back on again ¹³ _____ (see) what happens. He says that usually works.
A Yes, I remember ¹⁴ _____ (do) that the last time I had a problem, and it did work. But now my computer just refuses ¹⁵ _____ (start) up.
B Hmm. I think I know how ¹⁶ _____ (fix) it, but I need ¹⁷ _____ (take) the back off. I promise not ¹⁸ _____ (break) it …

c ⟫ Now go back to p. 96.

9A The passive

We form the passive using a form of *be* + past participle.

Active	09.03 Passive
They **make** a lot of movies in Hollywood.	A lot of movies **are made** in Hollywood.
The scriptwriters **are writing** a new script this week.	A new script **is being written** this week.
The real estate agent **has sold** the house for $1 million.	The house **has been sold** for $1 million.
There was an accident while they **were building** the bridge.	There was an accident while the bridge **was being built**.
A movie studio **will make** a movie from the book.	A movie **will be made** from the book.
Somebody **stole** our car during the night.	Our car **was stolen** during the night.
An expert **should do** the work.	The work **should be done** by an expert.

We use passive verb forms:
- when the main thing we are talking about is the object of the verb
  A movie **will be made** from the book.
  The work **should be done** by an expert. (We are talking about the work, not the expert.)
- when the agent (the doer) isn't important
  The house **has been sold** for $1 million. (We're not interested in the real estate agent.)
- when the agent (the doer) is very obvious
  A new script **is being written** this week. (by scriptwriters)
- when we don't know who did something / what caused something.
  Our car **was stolen** during the night.

Negatives and questions are made in the same way as other uses of *be*:
Movies **aren't** made here.
Is a movie **being** made here?

We use *by* to introduce the person or thing that did the action (the agent):
*This frame was drawn **by** one of the animators.*
We usually use *with* to introduce a tool, instrument, or technique that was used by the agent:
*The pirate's beard was controlled **with** a wire.*

> 🔖 **Tip**
> We can say something was made by hand or by machine:
> *This sweater was made **by hand** in Scotland.*

9B Defining and non-defining relative clauses

 09.07   **Defining and non-defining relative clauses**
Defining relative clauses define a noun or make it more specific. They tell us which particular thing or what kind of thing. In defining relative clauses, we can use *that*, *which*, or *who*:
*I love music **that/which makes people dance**.*
*I hate books **that/which don't have happy endings**.*
*My dad met the woman **who reads the news on TV** yesterday!*

Non-defining relative clauses often start with *which* or *who*. They give extra information about a noun, but they are not necessary for the sentence to make sense:
The DJ was playing hip-hop. (This sentence is complete.)
*The DJ was playing hip-hop, **which is my favorite kind of music**.* (This relative clause adds more information.)
My parents are from Honduras. (This sentence is complete.)
*My parents, **who came to the U.S. 20 years ago**, are from Honduras.* (This relative clause adds more information.)

In writing, we need a comma before and after a non-defining relative clause. Don't use commas in defining relative clauses:
*We visited the market on a **Sunday, when they sell clothes and jewelry**.*
*I met **Lucy, who was staying with relatives nearby**, for coffee.*

In both types of relative clause, we can use *who*, *which*, *whose*, *where*, and *when*. Don't use *that* in a non-defining relative clause.
*Have you been to **that restaurant where you cook your own food at the table**?*
*Did you meet **the girl whose father climbed Mt. Everest**?*

After *where*, we need to add a new subject to the relative clause. Compare:
*That's the shop **that sells** dictionaries.* (*that* is the subject of the relative clause)
*That's the shop **where you can buy** dictionaries.* (the relative clause has a new subject: you)

Omitting relative pronouns
We can often leave out *who/which/that* or *when* from defining relative clauses:
*He likes the cheese (**which/that**) I bought.*
(I bought the cheese. *cheese* = object)

Don't leave out the relative pronoun if it's the subject of the relative clause (*who*, *which*, or *that*):
*He likes the cheese **that** comes from Turkey.* (The cheese comes from Turkey. *cheese* = subject)

Never leave out the relative pronoun from a non-defining relative clause:
*This cheese, **which** Greg really likes, comes from Turkey.*
NOT *This cheese, Greg really likes, ...*

9A The passive

a Complete the passive sentences. Don't include any agents that are in parentheses.

1 Ryan Coogler directed *Black Panther*.   *Black Panther* _____ was directed by Ryan Coogler.
2 (People) still make these shoes by hand.   These shoes _____ are still made by hand.
3 (They) will build a new bridge next year.   A new _____
4 My grandfather gave me this watch.   I _____
5 (We)'ve told everybody to be here on time.   Everybody _____
6 (People) will laugh at you if you wear that hat.   You _____
7 A computer program creates the special effects.   The special effects _____
8 My parents are looking after our dog this week.   Our dog _____
9 (They) offered me $1,000 for my painting.   I _____
10 (Somebody) was repairing my car at the time.   My car _____

b Rewrite the sentences as either *Yes/No* questions (?) or negatives (–).

1 We were picked up at the airport.   (–) _____ We weren't picked up at the airport.
2 The painting's already been sold.   (?) _____ Has the painting already been sold?
3 The work will be finished by Saturday.   (–) _____
4 The movie's being made in Brazil.   (?) _____
5 Tomatoes are grown in Spain.   (?) _____
6 The car was being driven too fast.   (–) _____
7 The costumes were made by hand.   (?) _____
8 The sculpture has been taken to the museum.   (–) _____

c ≫ Now turn to p. 106.

9B Defining and non-defining relative clauses

a Complete the sentences with a word from the box. Sometimes more than one answer is possible. You will use some words more than once. Which sentence is also correct without a relative pronoun?

that   which   who   where   when   whose

1 I love people _____ can make me laugh.
2 I told Paula my secret, _____ she then told everyone!
3 The movie _____ I saw was really good.
4 Yesterday was the day _____ everything went wrong.
5 This album, _____ came out in 1967, has some great songs.
6 Mark is the person _____ father used to be a singer.
7 The store _____ I bought this T-shirt has closed now.
8 I met Sara, _____ husband I work with, yesterday.

b Rewrite the sentences, adding the information in parentheses as a non-defining relative clause. Use relative pronouns that refer to the underlined words.

1 Ariana Grande performed "No Tears Left to Cry." (She recorded it in 2018.)
   Ariana Grande performed "No Tears Left to Cry," which she recorded in 2018.
2 "Auld Lang Syne" is sung around the world on New Year's Day. (It was written by the poet Robert Burns.)
   _____
3 We're going to Cuba. (Mambo music comes from there.)
   _____
4 The Glastonbury Festival also has theater, comedy, and circus performances. (It's most famous as a music festival.)
   _____
5 My favorite singer is Beyoncé. (Her album *Lemonade* was released in 2016.)
   _____
6 The best day of the festival is the last day. (There's a big fireworks display then.)
   _____

c Rewrite the sentences, adding the information in parentheses as a defining relative clause. Leave out *who*, *which*, or *that* if possible.

1 I like the tune. (You were singing it.)
   I like the tune you were singing.
2 That's the DJ. (He was here two weeks ago.)
   _____
3 We need music. (It makes you want to dance.)
   _____
4 That's the stage. (We're going to perform there.)
   _____
5 I downloaded a new song. (You'll like it.)
   _____
6 What did you think of the music? (I chose it.)
   _____
7 What's the name of your friend? (You borrowed his earbuds.)
   _____
8 The song changed my life. (It's playing on the radio.)
   _____

d Are the sentences below correct (✓) or incorrect (✗)? Sometimes both sentences in a pair are correct.

1 a I like music that makes me dance. ✓
  b I like music makes me dance. ✗
2 a It's a drum that you play with your hands.
  b It's a drum you play with your hands.
3 a My father, that is a dentist, looks after my teeth.
  b My father, who is a dentist, looks after my teeth.
4 a This album, I bought last week, is really good.
  b This album, which I bought last week, is really good.

e ≫ Now turn to p. 108.

10A Present and future unreal conditionals

We use present and future unreal conditionals to talk about imagined events or states and their consequences. They can be about the unreal present or the unlikely future.

Real present		10.04 Unreal present and consequence
I don't know the answer.	→	*If I **knew** the answer, I**'d tell** you.*
Likely future		**Unlikely/imagined future and consequence**
She won't find out that you lied.	→	*She **would be** angry **if** she **found** out you had lied.*

We usually use the simple past in the *if*-clause and *would* in the main clause. We can use *could* or *might* instead of *would* to say that something is less likely:
*You **could afford** to go on vacation if you **were** more careful with your money.*
*If you **tried** harder, you **might win** a medal.*

The verb *be* can have a special form in present and future unreal conditionals. We can use *were* for all persons (*if I were, if you were, if she were*, etc.):
*If **I were** taller, I'd be better at basketball.*

We use the phrase *If I were you* to give advice:
***If I were you**, I wouldn't eat that fish. It doesn't smell fresh.*

We don't always need to include the *if*-clause if the meaning is clear:
*Look at that house! That **would** be a great place to live. (… if I moved there)*
*I'm sure Jack **would** help you. (… if you asked)*

> **Tip**
> When talking about the future, you can usually choose between the real and unreal future conditionals. Use the future real conditional if you think a future event is likely; use the future unreal conditional if you think it is unlikely.
> * *If we **score** one more point, we**'ll** win.*
>   (I think there's a good chance of this.)
> * *If we **scored** four more points, we**'d** win (but we probably won't).*

> **Tip**
> The contracted form of *would* (*'d*) is the same as the contracted form of *had*. You can tell the difference by looking at the verb that comes next.
> * *'d* + past participle: *He**'d won** (= had won) the match.*
> * *'d* + infinitive: *He**'d win** (= would win) the match.*

10B Past unreal conditionals

 10.08
We use past unreal conditionals to talk about imagined past events or states and their consequences:
*If you**'d told** me about your birthday, I **would have** bought you a present.*

We use the past perfect in the *if*-clause and *would have* + past participle in the main clause.

Real past		Unreal past and consequence
I didn't know the answer.	→	*If I**'d known** the answer, I**'d have done better** on the exam.*
Lou didn't work hard.	→	*If Lou **had worked** harder, he **would have earned** more money.*

We can also use *could have* or *might have* instead of *would have*:
*We **could have saved** some money **if** we**'d known** about the offer.*
***If** I **had done** more work, I **might have passed** the exam.*

Common uses of past unreal conditionals
1 Regrets about things that happened or didn't happen in the past:
  ***If** I**'d sold** my house two years ago, I**'d have made** a fortune.*
2 Relief about avoiding a past problem:
  *I **might have missed** the flight **if** you **hadn't woken** me up.*
3 Surprise about how things were different than expected:
  ***If** you**'d told** me five years ago I'd have my own company one day, I **wouldn't have believed** you.*

> **Tip**
> Be especially careful with the contraction *'d*. In the *if*-clause, it's a contraction of *had*. In the main clause, it's a contraction of *would*.

If you'd told me about your birthday, I'd have bought you a present.

10A Present and future unreal conditionals

a Match the sentence beginnings 1–8 with the most logical endings a–h.

1 If I had more money, [c]
2 I'd be grateful [ ]
3 If I were you, [ ]
4 If you asked her again nicely, [ ]
5 I wouldn't be so relaxed [ ]
6 If he weren't so rude, [ ]
7 I could get a better job [ ]
8 Angela would be really sad [ ]

a she might change her mind.
b more people would like him.
c I could eat in restaurants more often.
d if I spoke better English.
e if we didn't invite her.
f I'd complain to your boss.
g if you didn't tell anybody my secret.
h if I had an exam tomorrow!

b Underline the correct options.

1 *I'd go* / *I went* swimming more if *I'd have* / *I had* time.
2 If *I'd know* / *I knew* his number, *I'd call* / *I called* him.
3 *Would* / *Did* you mind if *I'd ask* / *I asked* you a question?
4 If you *wouldn't* / *didn't* have a car, how *would* / *did* you get around?
5 *You'd be* / *You were* a lot healthier if you *wouldn't* / *didn't* eat so much.
6 If *I'd be* / *I were* you, *I'd get* / *I got* some new shoes.
7 What *would* / *did* you do if *you'd see* / *you saw* a fire?
8 If someone *would treat* / *treated* you like that, how *would* / *did* you feel?

c Decide if a real or unreal conditional is more appropriate for each situation. Then complete the sentences with the correct form of the verbs in parentheses.

1 I think I'll probably leave my job soon. But if I _____leave_____ (leave) my job, it _____'ll be_____ (be) difficult to get a new one.
2 I think it's going to be a nice day. We _____ (can) have a picnic if the weather _____ (stay) nice.
3 I'm not very good at soccer. If I _____ (can) play better, I _____ (join) a soccer team.
4 If I _____ (win) the lottery, I _____ (buy) a new house. But I know it's never going to happen.
5 I think we're the best team. If we _____ (win) the competition, I _____ (not be) surprised.
6 You drink too much coffee. If you _____ (not drink) so much, you _____ (not be) so stressed.
7 She goes shopping all the time! She _____ (not have) any money left if she _____ (not stop) spending it!
8 I don't like my house in the city. If I _____ (live) in the country, I _____ (be) much happier.

d ≫ Now go back to p. 117.

10B Past unreal conditionals

a What does *'d* mean in each sentence? Write *had* or *would*.

1 If you'd (_had_) told me earlier, we'd (_would_) have saved a lot of time.
2 I don't know what I'd (_____) have done if you hadn't helped me.
3 We might have been seriously hurt if you'd (_____) crashed.
4 She'd (_____) have gotten the job if she'd (_____) applied for it.
5 I'd (_____) have loved to go to the party, but I wasn't invited.

b Write past unreal conditional sentences about the situations.

1 Real past: I didn't win the competition because I made a stupid mistake.
Unreal past: If I hadn't made a stupid mistake, I would have won the competition.
2 Real past: He went to live in Japan. While he was there, he met his wife.
Unreal past: If he _____
3 Real past: The car broke down, so we couldn't go to the concert.
Unreal past: We _____
4 Real past: I didn't go to see the movie because I didn't know it was so good.
Unreal past: I _____
5 Real past: You didn't take my advice, so you got lost.
Unreal past: If _____
6 Real past: You helped me so much. That's why I was so successful.
Unreal past: I wouldn't _____

c Find and correct the mistakes.

1 If you'd been there too, you would enjoy yourself.
_____would have enjoyed_____
2 We couldn't have bought the house if they wouldn't have lent us the money.
_____
3 If they hadn't noticed the fire, the whole house could burned down.
_____
4 If I know it was dangerous, I'd never have gone there.
_____
5 What you would have done if I hadn't helped you?
_____
6 He could have been an opera singer if he'd have some training.
_____
7 If they'd arrive a few minutes later, they might have missed you.
_____

d ≫ Now go back to p. 121.

Phonemic symbols

Vowel sounds

/ə/ umbrell**a**	/æ/ m**a**n	/ʊ/ p**u**t	/ɑ/ g**o**t
/ɪ/ ch**i**p	/i/ happ**y**	/e/ m**e**n	/ʌ/ b**u**t

/ɜ/ sh**ir**t	/ɑ/ p**ar**t	/u/ wh**o**	/ɔ/ w**a**lk

Diphthongs (two vowel sounds)

/eə/ h**air**	/ɪə/ n**ear**	/ɔɪ/ b**oy**	/ɑɪ/ f**i**ne	/eɪ/ late	/oʊ/ wind**ow**	/aʊ/ n**ow**

Consonants

/p/ **p**icnic	/b/ **b**ook	/f/ **f**ace	/v/ **v**ery	/t/ **t**ime	/d/ **d**og	/k/ **c**old	/g/ **g**o	/θ/ **th**ink	/ð/ **th**e	/tʃ/ **ch**air	/dʒ/ **j**ob
/s/ **s**ea	/z/ **z**oo	/ʃ/ **sh**oe	/ʒ/ televi**si**on	/m/ **m**e	/n/ **n**ow	/ŋ/ si**ng**	/h/ **h**ot	/l/ late	/r/ **r**ed	/w/ **w**ent	/j/ **y**es

Irregular verbs

Infinitive	Simple past	Past participle
be	was / were	been
become	became	become
begin	began	begun
blow	blew	blown
break	broke	broken
bring	brought	brought
build	built	built
buy	bought	bought
catch	caught	caught
choose	chose	chosen
come	came	come
cost	cost	cost
cut	cut	cut
deal	dealt	dealt
do	did	done
draw	drew	drawn
drink	drank	drunk
drive	drove	driven
eat	ate	eaten
fall	fell	fallen
feel	felt	felt
find	found	found
fly	flew	flown
forget	forgot	forgotten
get	got	gotten
give	gave	given
go	went	gone
grow	grew	grown
have	had	had
hear	heard	heard
hit	hit	hit
hold	held	held
keep	kept	kept
know	knew	known

Infinitive	Simple past	Past participle
leave	left	left
lend	lent	lent
let	let	let
lose	lost	lost
make	made	made
meet	met	met
pay	paid	paid
put	put	put
read	read	read
ride	rode	ridden
ring	rang	rung
run	ran	run
sit	sat	sat
say	said	said
see	saw	seen
sell	sold	sold
send	sent	sent
set	set	set
sing	sang	sung
sleep	slept	slept
speak	spoke	spoken
spend	spent	spent
stand	stood	stood
steal	stole	stolen
swim	swam	swum
take	took	taken
teach	taught	taught
tell	told	told
think	thought	thought
throw	threw	thrown
understand	understood	understood
wake	woke	woken
wear	wore	worn
win	won	won
write	wrote	written

Acknowledgments

The authors and publishers acknowledge the following sources of copyright material and are grateful for the permissions granted. While every effort has been made, it has not always been possible to identify the sources of all the material used, or to trace all copyright holders. If any omissions are brought to our notice, we will be happy to include the appropriate acknowledgments on reprinting and in the next update to the digital edition, as applicable.

Key
U = Unit, C = Communication, V = Vocabulary

Text
U1: Guardian News & Media Limited for the adapted text from "How I learned a language in 22 hours" by Joshua Foer, *The Guardian* 09.11.2012. Copyright © The Guardian. Reproduced with permission; **U4:** Guardian News & Media Limited for the adapted text from "Are you an introvert? Take our quiz," *The Guardian* 2012. Copyright © The Guardian. Reproduced with permission.

Photographs
The following photographs are sourced from Getty Images:
Front cover photography by Thomas Barwick/DigitalVision/Getty Images. **U6:** Matteo Colombo/Moment; Deimagine/E+; Imtmphoto/iStock/Getty Images Plus; FG Trade/E+; Olga Mazyarkina/iStock/Getty Images Plus; Mariha-kitchen/iStock/Getty Images Plus; Teen00000/iStock/Getty Images Plus; Mizina/iStock/Getty Images Plus; Sheri L Giblin/Photolibrary/Getty Images Plus; Nick Dolding/Stone; Mukesh-kumar/iStock/Getty Images Plus; Calvin Chan Wai Meng/Moment; John Seaton Callahan/Moment; Fazeful/iStock/Getty Images Plus; luchezar/E+; Thomas Barwick/Stone; imagenavi; Enes Evren/E+; Bruno De Hogues/Photographer's Choice/Getty Images Plus; Eloy Rodriguez/Moment; JazzIRT/E+; **U7:** Ed Freeman/Stone; Maica/iStock/Getty Images Plus; ExperienceInteriors/E+; Future Publishing; Wibowo Rusli/Lonely Planet Images/Getty Images Plus; Vostok/Moment; Canopy; ivo Gretener/iStock/Getty Images Plus; Jon Lovette/Stone; ArabianEye; Thomas Roche/Moment Open; Lonely Planet Images; Golibo/iStock; Jenny Jones/Lonely Planet Images/Getty Images Plus; Manoa/Moment; Photography by Deb Snelson/Moment; RiverNorthPhotography/iStock; AlexPro9500/iStock Editorial/Getty Images Plus; Jekaterina Nikitina/Stone/Getty Images Plus; Tim Robberts/DigitalVision; Portra/DigitalVision; Maskot; Mitchell Funk/Photographer's Choice/Getty Images Plus; Photographer's Choice; Bruce Weaver/AFP; Nisian Hughes/Stone; **U8:** Andre Ringuette/National Hockey League; Cavan Images; MEHDI FEDOUACH/AFP; 10'000 Hours/DigitalVision; Pekic/E+; Mixetto/E+; MStudioImages/E+; Eva-Katalin/E+; Liesel Bockl; FangXiaNuo/E+; FG Trade/E+; Colin Wilson/Moment; AntonioGuillem/iStock/Getty Images Plus; Santiago Urquijo/Moment; AzmanL/E+; Stock4Bcreative; **U9:** Perboge/iStock Editorial/Getty Images Plus; Westend61; Yiu Yu Hoi/The Image Bank; Erik Dreyer/Stone/Getty Images Plus; PeopleImages/E+; Ivan Jones/Stone/Getty Images Plus; David Redfern/Hulton Archive/Getty Images Plus; Hiroyuki Ito; Kevin Mazur/Getty Images Entertainment; Chris Mouyiaris/Robertharding/Getty Images Plus; Kiyoshi Ota/Getty Images Entertainment; PYMCA/Universal Images Group; Richard Newstead/The Image Bank; Rawpixel/iStock/Getty Images Plus; Ghislain & Marie David de Lossy/The Image Bank; AleksandarNakic/E+; Flashpop/DigitalVision; Uppercut; Martin-dm/E+; Robbie Jack/Corbis Entertainment; Frank van Delft/Cultura; Wayne Eastep/The Image Bank; Mark Andersen; Jeff Kravitz/FilmMagic, Inc; Hiroyuki Ito/Hulton Archive; **U10:** PeopleImages/E+; Technotr/E+; CHRISTOF STACHE/AFP; Bacalao64/iStock/Getty Images Plus; Jag_cz/iStock Editorial/Getty Images Plus; Frederic Pacorel/Photographer's Choice/Getty Images Plus; Mint Images-Steve Prezant; Trevor Williams/DigitalVision; Lorado/E+; Tom And Steve/Photographer's Choice/Getty Images Plus; FG Trade/E+; NDStock/iStock/Getty Images Plus; Fizkes/iStock/Getty Images Plus; Neale Clark/robertharding/Getty Images Plus; Image Source; Kupicoo/E+; Westend61; Morsa Images/DigitalVision; Musketeer/DigitalVision; Tim Hall/Cultura; Jamie Grill; Kieran Stone/Moment; SimonSkafar/E+; laflor/E+; **V:** Herianus Herianus/EyeEm; MB Photography/Moment; Yaorusheng/Moment; FEBRUARY/Moment; Boonchai wedmakawand/Moment; Didier Marti/Moment; Alison Taylor Photography/iStock/Getty Images Plus; FG Trade/iStock/Getty Images Plus; Michael Gebicki/Lonely Planet Images/Getty Images Plus; Robert Kneschke/EyeEm; Westend61; Paul Starosta/Stone; Ugurhan/E+; JillianSuzanne/iStock/Getty Images Plus; Mathieu/500px; MirasWonderland/iStock/Getty Images Plus; Christopher Furlong/Getty Images News.

The following images are sourced from other sources/libraries:
U6: Lucas Vallecillos/Alamy Stock Photo; © Dee and John Lee; **U8:** © Chris Bethell; **C:** © Chris Bethell; © Theo C. McInnes.

Commissioned photography by Gareth Boden.

Illustrations
QBS Learning; Beatrice Bencivenni; Mark Bird; Mark Duffin; Jo Goodberry; Mark (KJA Artists); Jerome Mireault; Gavin Reece; Gregory Roberts; Sean (KJA Artists); David Semple; Sean Sims; Marie-Eve-Tremblay.

Typeset by QBS Learning.

Audio Production by John Marshall Media.

Shaftesbury Road, Cambridge CB2 8EA, United Kingdom

One Liberty Plaza, 20th Floor, New York, NY 10006, USA

477 Williamstown Road, Port Melbourne, VIC 3207, Australia

314–321, 3rd Floor, Plot 3, Splendor Forum, Jasola District Centre, New Delhi – 110025, India

103 Penang Road, #05–06/07, Visioncrest Commercial, Singapore 238467

Cambridge University Press & Assessment is a department of the University of Cambridge.

We share the University's mission to contribute to society through the pursuit of
education, learning and research at the highest international levels of excellence.

www.cambridge.org
Information on this title: www.cambridge.org/9781108861571

First published 2022

20 19 18 17 16 15 14 13 12 11 10 9 8 7 6 5

Printed in Great Britain by CPI Group (UK) Ltd, Croydon CR0 4YY

A catalogue record for this publication is available from the British Library

ISBN 978-1-108-79807-5 Intermediate Student's Book with eBook
ISBN 978-1-108-79679-8 Intermediate Student's Book A with eBook
ISBN 978-1-108-79821-1 Intermediate Student's Book B with eBook
ISBN 978-1-108-86152-6 Intermediate Student's Book with Digital Pack
ISBN 978-1-108-86154-0 Intermediate Student's Book A with Digital Pack
ISBN 978-1-108-86157-1 Intermediate Student's Book B with Digital Pack
ISBN 978-1-108-79812-9 Intermediate Workbook with Answers
ISBN 978-1-108-79813-6 Intermediate Workbook A with Answers
ISBN 978-1-108-79814-3 Intermediate Workbook B with Answers
ISBN 978-1-108-79815-0 Intermediate Workbook without Answers
ISBN 978-1-108-79816-7 Intermediate Workbook A without Answers
ISBN 978-1-108-79817-4 Intermediate Workbook B without Answers
ISBN 978-1-108-79818-1 Intermediate Full Contact with eBook
ISBN 978-1-108-79819-8 Intermediate Full Contact A with eBook
ISBN 978-1-108-79820-4 Intermediate Full Contact B with eBook
ISBN 978-1-108-85951-6 Intermediate Full Contact with Digital Pack
ISBN 978-1-108-85952-3 Intermediate Full Contact A with Digital Pack
ISBN 978-1-108-86153-3 Intermediate Full Contact B with Digital Pack
ISBN 978-1-108-79823-5 Intermediate Teacher's Book with Digital Pack
ISBN 978-1-108-81765-3 Intermediate Presentation Plus

Additional resources for this publication at www.cambridge.org/americanempower

This page is intentionally left blank.

This page is intentionally left blank.